No Greater Jewel

Other books in the Lutheran Voices series

LUTHERAN
VOICES

No Greater Jewel
Thinking about Baptism
with Luther

Kirsi Stjerna

Augsburg Fortress

Minneapolis

Library of Congress Cataloging-in-Publication Data
Stjerna, Kirsi Irmeli, 1963-
    No greater jewel : thinking about baptism with Luther / Kirsi Stjerna.
        p. cm.—(Lutheran voices series)
    Includes bibliographical references (p.   ).
    ISBN 978-0-8066-8008-8 (alk. paper)
    1. Luther, Martin, 1483-1546. 2. Baptism—Lutheran Church. 3. Lutheran Church—Doctrines. I. Title.

    BR333.5.B3S75 2009
    234'.1610882841—dc22   2008050396

The paper used in this publication meets the minimum requirements of American National Standard for Information Sciences—Permanence of Paper for Printed Library Materials, ANSI Z329.48-1984.

Manufactured in the U.S.A.

13   12   11   10   09   1   2   3   4   5   6   7   8   9   10

*To my Brooks, to our children, and to our
parents and grandparents in Texas and Finland*

Contents

Preface

Usually when I entertain or feed my family, I load the table with food to make sure nobody leaves the table hungry. This is what happened with this book also. Originally proceeding with a vision to craft a "little book" on baptism, I found myself caught in a jet stream. All these delicious issues to cover! The mushrooming of ideas proves how central baptism is in Lutheran theology and spirituality. Thanks to Susan Johnson's editorial insights and Cynthia Nelson's careful copyediting, the manuscript finally landed in its current version.

With my Luther scholar colleagues' voices lurking in the background and my students' questions feeding my thoughts, I tried to keep in mind people like my parents: Lutherans seeking a deeper understanding on faith issues that matter to their hearts and daily lives. I wanted to lead readers to the heart of Luther's thinking and be inspired by the precious gems from the Luther quotes included in the text. I also wanted to invite readers to appropriate Lutheran beliefs in light of the bigger picture of the history of Christian practices and the global networks of believers of different faiths.

I am indebted to mentors with whom I have had the privilege to study Luther's works: Dr. Tuomo Mannermaa from Finland who dared to conclude that Lutheran theology of justification has missed much by ignoring Luther's understanding of human beings becoming one with Christ in justification, a finding that holds tremendous spiritual and ecumenical promise; Dr. Carter Lindberg from Boston University who modeled a way to interpret Luther's teachings and input with authenticity in his own historical context and theological framework and in light of his pastoral and fatherly sensitivities; Dr. Eero Huovinen, Bishop of Helsinki, who for decades has been lifting up the gem of Luther's baptismal theology—that infants may believe just as well, if not better, than anybody else. I am also grateful for the inspiration of my colleagues at the Lutheran Theological Seminary at Gettysburg, Dr. Kristin Johnston

Largen and, most of all, Dr. Brooks Schramm who have significantly shaped my thinking about baptism in relation to people practicing other faiths.

The original stimulus for this book came from my seminary students and my children, as well as from the many children I have had the privilege to baptize. My children, since their births in the United States and their baptisms in Finland, have invoked my thoughts about the necessity of baptism and about the many channels of God's grace in children's lives in particular. They have also provided much side material with their questions about baptism and their attempts to baptize all kinds of God's creatures, dead or alive!

Many of the endnotes originally crafted to support the text ended up in the desk drawer. Some suggestions for further reading are listed at the back of this book, and they also indicate my sources. Two books have been most important. First, David Spinks's illuminating studies on baptism through the Christian centuries are the backbone for my historical information. Second, Timothy Lull's edition of *Martin Luther's Basic Theological Writings*—the source for most of my Luther quotations—includes a variety of important texts that are available in the multi-volume American edition of Luther's works but compiled and revised in Lull's book, especially in regard to gendered language.

A word about the gendered language: Not wanting to change Luther's words or intents, I have, whenever possible and the least obstructive, substituted male pronouns in brackets or simply added a [sic] to indicate where better wording would be desired. There was no space to sufficiently deal with the delicate issue of what language we use about God, especially regarding the Trinitarian "male-sounding" language that is at the heart of baptismal rituals. The issue of gender and God-language remains important for us, but was not on Luther's radar screen. His utmost concern was that we "know" God—of whom he used a fresh repertoire of images—rather than what words and names we use for God, who escapes our constructions anyway.

I dedicate this book to my family, especially to my parents by birth and by marriage, Sirkka and Alho (+) Stjerna, Finland, and Lynn and

Bennie Schramm, Texas. I thank from the bottom of my heart my family for their patience and inspiration. Most of all, I thank my husband, Brooks Schramm. I hope that our "little" Kristian and Kaleigh Kirsikka, who daily remind us of the power of forgiveness and love, one day will appreciate the words offered in this small book.

Introduction:
"No Greater Jewel"

"How many of you remember when you were baptized?" the pastor asked the children gathered around her during one of the weekly children's sermons. Some children raised their hands and recited dates or other memories. Those who had been baptized as older children had more to share. At the close of the sermon, the pastor challenged the children to find out all they could about their baptisms and to share their baptismal dates with the church office so this important event could be acknowledged in the church bulletin and celebrated communally every year. A child, sitting in the pew, too old for "children's time," whispered loudly into her mother's ear, "What's the big deal with the baptismal date? Isn't my birthday more important?"

Now that is a good question: What does the date matter? Or why does the ritual matter? Martin Luther would say it matters quite a lot.

During his career in Wittenberg, Martin Luther (1483–1546), a sixteenth-century German reformer known as the father of the Lutheran church, spent much time thinking about baptism. Baptized on St. Martin's day—hence his name—and a baptizer of many, Luther remained intrigued throughout his life by the mystery of the sacrament. He wrote in his *Large Catechism,* an educational tool for parish pastors published in 1529: "In baptism, therefore, every Christian has enough to study and practice all his or her life. Christians always have enough to do to believe firmly what baptism promises and brings—victory over death and the devil, forgiveness of sin, God's grace, the entire Christ, and the Holy Spirit with his [sic] gifts. In short, the blessings of baptism are so boundless that if our timid nature considers them, it may well doubt whether they could all be true."[1]

In these few words the reformer affirmed the power of baptism and offered reasons for thoughtfully and intentionally remembering our baptisms. According to Luther, nothing less is given in baptism than holiness. In baptism, nothing less is given than transforming forgiveness and a foundation for a new life, a new start for every new day. In baptism, nothing less is given than God—not part of God but full God, our Creator, Redeemer, and Sanctifier who connects with us in person in a way that makes our life Spirit-filled and, thus, spiritual. In baptism, nothing less is given than the promise of a spiritually meaningful and conscious life rooted in God in this world and beyond. According to Luther, "No greater jewel, therefore, can adorn our body and soul than baptism, for through it we become completely holy and blessed, which no other kind of life and no work on earth can acquire."[2] Plenty of reasons, surely, for us to remember the date when all this became true "for us"—"for me"!

That is where the rubber hit the road for Luther and for his contemporaries, and that is where the issues around baptism crystallize for us: the personal meaning of baptism "for us" and the actual reaping of the benefits of baptism in our physical lives together. Throughout his career, Luther dealt extensively with the doctrinal issues and practical dilemmas that followed the changes he introduced to rectify some of the central teachings and practices of the medieval Catholic church according to his "re-newed" understanding of the intent of the gospel message (thus the label "evangelicals" or "protestants" for those who followed Luther). Luther's main concern with baptism in particular remained most of all spiritual—the godly meaning and effects of baptism in our lives. Never just an issue of doctrine or only an external practice, baptism is a personal matter about our relationship with God in the deepest level of our being. To Luther, baptism was a matter of intimacy with God and finding oneself in that relationship, while at the same time, it never remained solely a private matter. Quite the contrary: as a spiritually transformative event, baptism for Luther promised changes in the lives lived with others as well. Baptism for Luther was a beginning of spiritual—or Spirit-filled—life and, as such, it was something quite incredible.

Today the word *spirituality* has quite diverse connotations, and Luther did not use the word as we do. But with all his talk about

Spirit-filled life he certainly offered a particular view that we can actually talk about as "Luther's spirituality" or "Lutheran spirituality." In a nutshell, Luther's vision of spirituality revolved around how God the Spirit comes to us, lives in us, and guides us and how we can invite the Spirit's presence into our lives, seeking to better appreciate it and become instruments of the Spirit in this life. Spirituality is about the intentional search for the godly purpose and meaning of our lives, being conscious of the ways we connect with our creator and one another, and the increasing sense of wholeness as spiritual and bodily creatures whose lives have a divine design. In his teaching of baptism, Luther invited his fellow seekers to a life-long journey of reaping the benefits of a spiritual gem given in water and Word, focused on God as the source of happiness.

As a spiritual sign and a starting point for spiritual living, baptism is tied essentially to the life of the church, the spiritual home where baptism is celebrated and taught with history and shared faith behind it. Baptism's benefits are personal, but it is also a public act and one of the essential signs and gifts of the church and its ministry in the world. For Luther's contemporaries, this was one of the sticking points: given all the changes in religious life introduced by the reformers, how would the "new church" administer and teach about the sacrament of baptism that had been one of the cornerstones of Christian identity and communities for centuries? Today we are revisiting the very issue in our context where more diverse practices of Christianity and Christian baptism abound than Luther could have ever imagined. What exactly are our hopes regarding baptism, and what might our concerns be as individuals and as a church?

With Luther as our guide, we can seek the meaning of baptism for us personally, to find ways to experience and live out the meaning of this symbol of God's presence in our lives. With Luther as our guide, we can seek to reimagine the purpose and potential consequences of baptism in the life of the church and in the lives of all the baptized, and thus in the world where Christians embody (or should embody) a particular message of God's love and grace and justice. With Luther we can rethink exactly what we believe about and teach about baptism and with what hopes we teach. With Luther as our guide, we can take a fresh look at the "jewel" passed on to us.

Like the child in the pew we can ask for ourselves: Why does remembering our baptismal date matter, or does it? We can start by seeking wisdom from the Christian past.

1

Why and How Have Christians Baptized?

Why Baptize?

Baptism has always centered on the life and work of Jesus Christ. The Gospels of Matthew, Mark, and Luke tell us that Jesus himself was baptized by John the Baptist in the Jordan River. We baptize because Jesus was baptized. Moreover, we baptize because of his command: "Go therefore and make disciples of all nations, baptizing them in the name of the Father and of the Son and of the Holy Spirit" (Matt. 28:19). So Christians have done, with much passion and zeal, since the time of Jesus. But there is still another reason why we baptize. We baptize because of what we believe and what Christians before us believed about Jesus and his promises to those baptizing in his name: "Remember, I am with you always" (Matt. 28:20). Why baptize? We baptize because of Jesus' example, by his command, and trusting in his promise. We baptize because we want Jesus' presence to continue in our lives and we desire all the blessing of God that follows from that. But, as we shall see, how that plays out through history is not nearly so tidy.

A Matter of Identity for the Followers of Jesus

For the earliest followers of Jesus, baptism was first and foremost an issue of identity, a personal and a public matter. Baptism meant becoming a Christian—a Christ-follower—one who followed in the footsteps and in the teachings of Jesus and gathered around his memory. In a public ritual, a family or an individual joined the followers of Jesus. The baptized lost his or her Jewish identity or his or her identity as a Roman believer in ancient gods and assumed a new identity altogether, with a worldview and values that were alien to those outside the Christian community. Immersion in the water of baptism granted a new identity—an identity linked to Christ.

Eager to keep Jesus' memory and promise alive—and to continue to experience ritualistically his presence—the early Christians went on to baptize, extending an invitation to all: Jews, Romans, Greeks; men, women, and children. In the community of the baptized, they were one body, united in their faith and hope and mission of love in the name of Jesus. In the first decades, baptism gave Christian communities a sense of belonging, a sense of togetherness they needed, most dramatically, during times of persecution when openly confessing Jesus as Lord put a person and entire family in jeopardy.

Why was baptism such a risky enterprise? In baptism one embraced a new religion that offended many of the sensitivities of the people in antiquity. In baptism one confessed a faith that, at first, did not have the approval of the authorities and was not protected by the law. From the time of Jesus' death until the emperor Constantine in the fourth century, Christians suffered from periodic, recurring, and at times intense persecutions, depending on the current emperor's preferences and attitudes toward Christians and their religion. Most radically, in baptism one accepted a view of God who cared personally about every human being, so much that God had taken on flesh and blood and come to live among us in the person of Jesus of Nazareth. This was simply unheard of and strange. Also disturbing was the fact that during his brief ministry, Jesus had spoken often of the unfathomable nature of God's love and demonstrated such love through healing and embracing those who were outcast by society. In the end, his scandalous message of love proclaimed through word and deed cost him his life, and that became the greatest story of godly love. Jesus' followers continued to baptize in his name, calling all the baptized to teach Jesus' radical message of God's love and his command and example to love one's neighbors and enemies alike. In seeking to live according to Jesus' example, they exposed themselves to the dangers of being rejected, ridiculed, and even killed, just as had happened to Jesus.

As expansively as the early Christians offered the "Jesus baptism," they also soon formed specific prerequisites about who could be baptized and when. Those seeking to be baptized were expected to confess their acceptance of certain principal "truths" about Jesus as Christ: that he was the child of God, that he was truly human and truly God, that he died and was resurrected, that he would come again to claim his kingdom, and that those baptized in his name would be included in his resurrection and life after death. Those to be baptized were educated in these beliefs and were also questioned about these beliefs being meaningful to them personally.

Baptism Rituals Observed in the Early Church

Few sources exist about the actual baptismal practices of the early church in the centuries between Jesus (first century) and church father Augustine (fourth/fifth century). Beyond scattered mention in the New Testament about baptismal rituals or the more formulaic "creedal" words used among the new generations of Christians,[1] there is no standard text or ritual available for us to study; there was hardly any available at the time either. Instead of rigid uniformity, there is evidence of significant local variance, with some basic commonalities and shared principles such as the use of water and reference to Jesus' words, and, quite early on, a creedal statement about the Trinity. It seems that early Christians enjoyed a certain amount of freedom in regard to how to conduct baptisms and with what emphasis. Over the generations, diverse elaborate rituals evolved from the simple baptism of Jesus in the Jordan River and the hasty secret baptisms performed during times of persecution.

What sources we have available let us believe that after the storm calmed down, when baptism moved from underground and behind closed doors to an open Sunday service, focus was more on the beauty of the ritual and its observance and less on baptismal doctrine and theology. Detailed attention was given to baptismal practice and reverent observance of the ritual. Sources indicate that intentional pre-baptism teaching focused on understanding the holiness and meaningful symbolism of the ritual that took place, and it was seen as a highlight in the life of the church receiving new members.

Just looking at the details we have available about the earliest institutionalized baptismal rituals is revealing, at least for two reasons. First, there have been shifts in emphasis about the meaning of baptism. Second, flexibility amidst changes has characterized the development of baptismal practices over time. Both of these observations are of worth to us in our efforts to redefine the meaning of baptism for us and for others and the parameters for its practice in changing contexts. The wisdom from the past, generally speaking, does not seem to condone a rigid set-in-stone model of baptism to be applied in all places and at all times. One more observation can be made: the ritual has curiously shrunk over the centuries.

For example, according to Hippolytus, a third-century priest in Rome who wrote about the rite used in his "congregation," the ritual was much more elaborate than we know it today. Typically there would be a prayer over the water and flowing water was used. The ritual included kissing the forehead of the baptized and anointing the baptized with oil. Women and men were separated, as they proceeded to the ritualistic removal of clothes, loosening of hair, and removal of jewelry. The symbolism of nudity was important for the ritualized new birth, as was exorcism—driving out of the evil spirits—and the bishop's laying of the hands on the baptized. (The first two became more contested as time went by, the third evolved into a separate "confirmation" ritual, due to the difficulty of having a bishop available for each baptism. Bishops were busy people already in the early church!) The liturgy included infant baptism but, at the same time, had at center stage a thorough preparation of the candidates with catechesis and interrogation, that is, education on the basics of Christian beliefs. Fasting and a days-long final preparation for baptism would conclude with an anointment with oil.[2]

Baptism in the life of the early church was much more than a Sunday ceremony. It involved community participation and deliberate preparation of the candidates for a ritual that was held in the highest esteem. Obviously, things have changed a lot from those days. For one, there definitely are no nude baptisms practiced in Lutheran circles today, nor is pre-baptism instruction standardized or even required.

In fact, today we tend to put more emphasis on educating members toward confirmation, with much variety there as well. The baptism liturgy has been simplified considerably, making it possible to celebrate baptisms during a standard hour-long worship service, as is generally the practice in most Northern American Lutheran churches today. (As a point of curiosity, let it be stated that different preferences prevail in other parts of the world. For instance in Scandinavian countries, home baptisms are far more common.)

What happened between the practices of the early church and our day? For one, the European Reformations happened. Also before that, serious formative work in the theological arena shaped the church's teaching of baptism and what was considered essential and what was less important for the ritual, in light of its simple origins.

A most important interpreter and definer of Christian faith was St. Augustine, bishop of Hippo (died 430 c.e.). He shaped Christians' thinking about baptism more than any other theologian. Before Augustine, baptism had been considered primarily as a ritual of being baptized "into" God's community and into the eschatological (future) life-after-death community of God and other believers. Due to Augustine's influence, the ritual became increasingly seen as a means of purification and forgiveness "from" sin and all that binds. Augustine portrayed human nature as being tied to sin from birth, and thus in need of God's irresistible ways of grace. He lifted up baptism as a means of grace. Lifting up the gifts of baptism, Augustine came to conclude that un-baptized persons, even infants, would not be saved.[3]

Largely due to Augustine's influence, the Christian church came to prefer infant baptism. Even the canon law applied throughout Christendom during the Middle Ages came to dictate that all citizens needed to be baptized and in a timely manner (typically within eight days from birth). While the reasons for infant baptism were theological, the consequences of not adhering to the rule were sometimes legal. This issue was revisited at the time of the Reformation because of the Anabaptists who, for theological reasons, digressed from this rule and preferred adult "believers' baptism."

Doctrines Defined in the Middle Ages

Christian thinking about baptism has evolved along with church doctrine about the basics of Christian beliefs: what Christians believe about the Trinity; how Christians understand human nature and life in its limitations and possibilities in sight of eternity; what is meant by sin, grace, and salvation; and what the role of the church is in Christians' lives and in the world. It was important for Christians, who were increasingly plagued by splits among them, to clarify with what words to proclaim the message of divine restoration to the world. Before agreeing on "what was broken and how it could be fixed," Christians struggled to see eye-to-eye on how to understand and talk about God. This was important, for the validity of any rituals practiced in the name of Christian faith, such as baptism, would depend on the "right" understanding of God—Christ's person in particular.

The famous Council of Nicaea (325 c.e.) called by the Emperor Constantine marked the watershed and most notable attempt to gain some imperial and churchly control over what was being taught and practiced. The ensuing other so-called ecumenical councils of the church, held between the fourth and eighth centuries, defined what was to be the "orthodox" line of teaching for the whole church on issues that mattered the most, such as baptism.[4] Those decisions were reached by a majority of voices coming mostly from the Eastern bishops' ranks and did not officially include the concerns of the laity or women. They carry weight even today, as we regularly recite those beliefs in the words of the creeds in worship and in baptismal rituals.

While early church writers had focused their attention on the description and meaning of the ritual of baptism, during the Middle Ages the doctrinal issues moved increasingly to the center of the discussion. With no efficient mechanism to supervise and control every local religious *practice*, some diversity could still be tolerated in the expanding world of Christendom, but when it came to *teaching* and *doctrine*, the church made a significant effort toward uniformity and clarity. What ultimately is baptism about? How does it work and why? How is it used right by the church? These were some of the questions that led the medieval church to declare baptism a sacrament.

Sacraments were defined on the basis of criteria originally set forth by Augustine: when Word is joined with the element, such as water in baptism, there is a sacrament, and as such it has the power to convey grace. This definition would later be revisited, during the Protestant Reformations. During the Middle Ages seven sacraments were identified for the church to have at its disposal to mediate God's grace in this world. The seven sacraments managed by the clergy included Baptism, the Lord's Supper, Confirmation, Confession, the Last Ointment, Marriage, and Ordination. These were affirmed officially in the Fourth Lateran Council (1215 c.e.) and reaffirmed at the Council of Trent (1545–1563), against the Protestants' explicit suggestion of the validity of only two sacraments—Baptism and the Lord's Supper.

In medieval discussion, the emphasis shifted from observing the ritual and its symbolic meaning to give increased attention to "what else" happens—what happens in the invisible realm of things. Everything that was discussed or decided about baptism had its basis in the decisions of the early church regarding who God is and how God's gifts come to us in the work and person of Jesus Christ. The simple example of Jesus being baptized and commissioning his followers to do the same had exploded into a complex web of beliefs about the nature of divinity and the ability or disability of human beings to connect with what is of and from God. Baptism offered a venue to sort this out around a practice that brought all these beliefs down to the life of "ordinary" believers who brought themselves and their children to baptism with great hopes.

For more than three centuries, theologians such as Peter Lombard (died 1160), Thomas Aquinas (died 1274), Bonaventure (died 1274), Duns Scotus (died 1308), and Gabriel Biel (died 1495) contributed to the church's understanding of the meaning of baptism and of sacraments in general. Amidst different emphases, their common concern was to explain the mechanics of the sacrament as a tool for salvation and for the removal of sin. They deliberated on the role of faith versus the role of ceremony in effecting and receiving the promised benefits; that is, would a person's faith make a difference or was the sacrament effective by the act of ritual itself? The use of the Trinitarian formula was re-affirmed as theologians drew a deliberate connection between baptism and what it meant to be an image of God. Baptism was considered a major connection point in time where we as finite and mortal human persons could encounter the eternal, infinite, unlimited God in Trinity, in whose image we were created in the first place. In baptism, the Creator's intent comes true and the Holy Trinity connects with us in specific ways.

There was less disagreement about *whether* the Holy Trinity connected with human persons in baptism and more headaches over *how* this took place. The theologians' inexhaustible explanations for how exactly the sacrament of baptism worked were part of their efforts to imagine grace and God's mediation of divine gifts and assistance to human beings in ways we could experience. Discussion about grace meant diving deeper into the whole question of the meaning of sin—what separates us from God and goodness and what causes suffering and distress, interrupting our creator's benign intents. Both topics—grace and sin—inspired sophisticated theological explanations about salvation matters. For instance, different degrees of sin were imagined, with different remedies for each; likewise, different degrees of grace were imagined, as were particular means for receiving that grace. The use of sacraments was taught within this kind of theological framework.

In medieval teaching, generally speaking, the emphasis in baptism was on washing away the guilt and shame caused by the "original" inherited sin that affected every newborn after the first fall of Adam and Eve in the Garden of Eden. From baptism on, persons received different degrees of grace through the other sacraments in order to fight the remaining kindle of sin that drew them to do and desire wrong, against the intent and desire of God the creator. In a lifelong battle against this twisted impulse, persons could expect to be given grace like a divine booster shot, receiving it in varying degrees. They could find forgiveness and healing from the so-called venial sins (minor transgressions that could be forgiven), whereas mortal sins were those acts that were, as the name implied, unforgivable. Because of the reality of sin and its burdens, the sacraments were of crucial importance. Because of the gospel about God's grace embodied in Christ and because of the authority given to the church and particularly its rightly ordained clergy as officiants, sacraments were considered potent and effective.

An important conclusion was made in the height of the Middle Ages about the absolute effectiveness of the sacraments regardless of the person's worth or goodness or even the intent of the one administering it. It was believed that the sacrament was effective purely from *ex opere operato*, which means, by the mere fact of being performed correctly by a rightly authorized and ordained clergy person. This degree emphasized the source of grace—God—and underscored the true effectiveness of the words and the materials used. The foundation for this belief was in the assertions of Augustine, who had given the Christian church a terminology for how to talk about sacraments and whose views on inherited sin and of the irresistible grace were at the root of how the sacraments were used in the medieval church. His teaching had laid the roots for the church's idiosyncratic teaching of the sacrament of baptism as a necessary act. Augustine's views were revisited during the Protestant Reformations, when Martin Luther approached the issue of baptism from the point of view of people—men and women concerned about their fate and the fate of their children.[5]

The Salvation Issue

The issue Martin Luther faced—and inherited—first and foremost was the church's teaching that baptism was the only way to salvation and that there were no other saving means outside the Christian church. Looking back, from where did this conviction come?

When early Christians baptized, they baptized newcomers into a community that was preparing for the kingdom of God that Jesus had preached about and that was waiting for Christ's promised return. There was an expectation of seeing Jesus face to face. Being members of the community of Jesus would ensure that. Fairly early on, Christians began to teach that those not belonging to the visible community of Christians on earth would not be included in the coming fulfillment of the invisible kingdom of God in the unknown future either. In other words, those who were not baptized would not be "saved." They would live and die without Jesus, apart from God and

God's blessings. One was either "in" or "out" of the Christian community (in this world as well as in the life to come), and baptism was the sign of that. Furthermore, imperial legislation mandating baptism placed those not baptized outside both the church and the Christian empire. The scary alternative—if one was even imagined—was finding a place outside the "only" world known to most people—the Christian West! Today we live in a very different situation.[6]

Two developments were coinciding: Christian teaching about baptism tightened, and the church became increasingly institutionalized and secure as a force and structure in society. In an effort to homogenize the religious practices that for long had had their own local flavor, the church began to assume tighter control over the means of grace as well. In the Middle Ages, doctrinal uniformity was valued more than diversity in local observance of the baptismal ritual. Baptism and what it offered remained the cornerstone of the Christian church. Moreover, it became the very central "key to the kingdom" in the hands of the church. The church preached and offered baptism as a necessary ritual for salvation and inclusion to the kingdom of God (that the church represented in this world). This development coincided the enhancement of the institutional authority of the church and its clergy, including the ballooning of the papal office at the top, from where such official statements could come as salvation being tied to the hands of the papal-led church. These were some of the issues that excited Martin Luther once he began to revisit the basic issue of salvation—from what people were saved, and by what means and authority. Once Luther began to question whether the traditions of his church were faithful to the model of the early Christians and the teachings of Jesus, he needed to pause and reflect on what message the church had the right to offer and if its current message really reached the people and met their spiritual needs. Many of the issues that surfaced had to do with baptism.

Baptism and Children

In the medieval church in the centuries preceding Luther, children's baptism was more of a norm than an exception. This was so primarily because the law under the rule of a Christian emperor and the pope as the head of the church demanded baptism of new citizens in a timely manner; the issue of baptism as a "choice" had become more or less a moot issue. But when exactly did infant baptism begin and is it really the most authentic form of baptism? These questions have been frequently asked even today.

In the early church, whole households—including both adults and children—typically were baptized. In later centuries, it was children who were usually welcomed to baptism in the catholic Christian church, following Jesus' invitation "Let the children come." Looking at Jesus' model and preaching, infant baptism seems logical, even if Jesus himself was baptized as an adult, as were his first followers. Looking at the rituals from the early church, certain parts indicate that deliberate learning of the new faith was presumed and thus would imply adult baptism, while not necessarily excluding infant baptism. There is much disagreement on the matter today, in regard to what is the more "original" practice or what would be the most prudent age for baptizing, as is evidenced by the diverse practices of various Christian denominations and the different theological interpretations of scripture regarding baptism. The question is not a new one; indeed, theologians have been deliberating on this issue for centuries.

Augustine, for instance, did not explicitly promote infant baptism as such. At the same time, he gave all the theological reasons for baptizing infants in his vision about the universally experienced real presence of sin: even the "little sinners" needed the purification offered in baptism. One of Augustine's main concerns was exorcism, the concrete purification of the baptized from the power of "evil," which the ritual itself would effect. Theologians in the Middle Ages developed Augustine's legacy, and the church more deliberately continued to teach the urgency of infant baptism, as a norm rather than an exception.

During the Reformation Era, the case for infant baptism and the issue of choice was reopened, due in great part because of the Anabaptists who began to preach and practice baptism as a demonstration and an oath of one's faith, best professed as a committed adult. This jeopardized them in a serious way as they not only were teaching against centuries of Christian doctrine on the meaning of a sacrament and the role of the church in meting out means of salvation, but they were also breaking the law. As in so many other matters, Luther was called to respond and redefine what baptism actually meant for Christians, for Protestants, "for us." Should the children born to Protestant families be baptized, and if so, why and how? The bottom line was, and still is, why should anyone be baptized—especially if Luther's conclusion is correct, that grace is free? Why, indeed?

For Reflection and Discussion

1. Why did the early Christians baptize? What was at stake for them?

2. Why do we baptize? What is at stake for us? Are there any risks involved?

3. In light of the history of Christian baptism, what is essential in baptism? How much flexibility and openness to variety and changes is there in the Christian church's teaching and practice of baptism?

4. How well do our current practices help us celebrate the two historically celebrated dimensions of baptism: being forgiven and liberated "from" all that binds, and being immersed and invited "into" a new life and community? Is this symbolism enough and meaningful for us? Is there anything else we could celebrate in baptism?

2

Luther and Luther's Writings on Baptism

Luther, the Reformer

Before considering Martin Luther's writings, a brief overview of Luther's role in the European Reformations seems in order. Luther (1483–1546) was an Augustinian monk and a professor at the Wittenberg University in Saxony, Germany, who rose to fame after posting ninety-five theses on the castle church door in Wittenberg, questioning some of the malpractices and corruption in the church at the time. His main concern was that people were being sold forgiveness and promises of salvation on false premises and for a fee. He was bothered by church teachings and practices that indicated grace came with a price tag or that put an unnecessary yoke on people already burdened by uncertainty in the face of omnipresent death, while at the same time bishops and the pope were elevated to a status beyond reproach.

Luther's criticisms echoed in the hearts of many and escalated into not only academic debates but also enforced cries and attempts for wide reform. In 1518, the monk had to explain what he had been "up to" in a hearing with his fellow monks. This gathering resulted in one of his most poignant arguments, published as the *Heidelberg Disputation*, about the foolishness of human wisdom and our lack of freedom, and, most importantly, about the nature of "true theology" that emerged from the experience of suffering like Christ. In 1520, he outlined a program for reform, calling on the German princes and leaders to join him in defending the gospel and openly "correcting" his church's teaching of the sacraments and its overemphasis on the power of the pope and the rest of the clergy. He proposed a vision for Christian life in freedom with a responsibility to love as a result of being liberated by faith. To no surprise, in 1521, the provocative professor was called to recant at the Diet of Worms, in front of the emperor and the German princes. He refused and from there on lived the life of an excommunicated outlaw in the eyes of the church and the Empire. Followed by an increasing number of scholars, clergy, and laity from within and beyond German territories, Luther continued to spearhead reformations, with several Protestant princes eager to defend the new preaching and the practice of "evangelical" faith.

From 1521 on, others implemented Luther's views in earnest even more hastily than the reformer would have preferred. In 1530, the "evangelicals" presented to the emperor and the German princes *The Augsburg Confession*, crafted by Phillip Melanchthon in collaboration with other reformers. It offered a public defense of the evangelical views, but it was rejected. It took until 1555 for the Lutheran theology, with rights to worship, to be legally accepted. In 1580, *The Book of Concord* was published, containing the official Lutheran theology that became the basis for the Lutheran tradition that continues to hold authority for Lutherans worldwide even today.

Until his dying day Luther continued to write treatises that addressed emerging issues, from childbirth and the Black Plague to the need to educate youth, establish welfare systems, and teach the "right" doctrine of the sacraments. He wrote several commentaries and translations of the Scriptures and published many of his sermons. Among his most influential texts today stand his 1529 Catechisms, his 1537 summation called the *Smalcald Articles* (included in *The Book of Concord*), and his 1520 and 1525 works, *On Christian Freedom* and *The Bondage of the Will*. Of his biblical works, three in particular deserve to be lifted up: his lectures on Genesis from the end of his life and his commentaries on Paul's letters to the Romans and the Galatians. The latter Luther called fondly his "Katharina von Bora," after the mother of his children whom he married in 1525, an act that culminated many of the Protestant Reformation principles and ideals about the godly purposes and blessings of human life.

Luther's Central Texts about Baptism

Throughout his career, Luther defended the sacrament of baptism from the pulpit and in writing. During the first years of reforms, however, while his attention was divided between many emerging issues regarding church practices and teachings, baptism was not on the front burner. It simply was not one of the hotly debated issues that demanded his immediate attention. However, it became more urgent after confrontation with another, more radical branch of Protestants, the so-called Anabaptists. This group professed "believer's baptism" and rejected the orthodox practice of baptizing infants, which by this time was required by law. The Anabaptists, more than any other "conversation partner" of Luther, served as a stimulus for Luther to clarify exactly what he and his followers taught about baptism as a means of grace and about its meaning in the life of the individual as well as in the life of the church. Luther argued for the purpose of sacraments in the first place and for the wisdom of infant baptism specifically, in response to the Anabaptists' differing opinions about whether either was necessary. He also addressed the issue of how faith matters in his 1528 treatise *Concerning Re-baptism*. The issues and arguments in that treatise echo the fundamental differences we see today between the baptismal theologies of Lutherans and of so-called charismatic or fundamentalist Christians.

One of Luther's earliest and most important texts on baptism is his *Baptismal Booklet* from 1523. In it Luther explained the meaning of the sacrament and the specific ritual he deemed appropriate. Even before that, in 1519, he had written *The Holy and Blessed Sacrament of Baptism*. Ten years later, Luther took on the explicit task of interpreting the meaning of the sacraments to both laity and clergy in his most widely read works, *The Small Catechism* and *The Large Catechism* respectively. He saw as a central part of basic Christian education the need to teach people the meaning of the sacraments and their right use by the church and to stimulate their appropriate appreciation by the individual. Luther felt this happened best in conjunction with educating Christians on the deeper meaning of the Ten Commandments, the Creeds, and the Lord's Prayer—all tools given to foster the spiritual life and wellbeing of the baptized. Luther's later summation of his theology, the *Smalcald Articles*, re-enforced the arguments already well stated in his Catechisms, showing how little had changed in his theology of baptism over time.

Central Themes and Perspectives on Baptism

The continuity in the teachings of the young Luther and the mature Luther regarding baptism can be explained from his enduring basic understanding of the relationship between God and humankind. When interpreting Scripture from its original languages, Luther underscored, on the one hand, human beings' inability to save themselves because of sin, and on the other hand, his re-discovery of the gospel message that human beings become pleasing to God by God's grace and by faith alone. From this standpoint he taught baptism and its necessity and right use in the life of the Christian community of believers. He saw baptism through the lens of how he understood grace and justification and vice versa. Without his doctrine of justification—his understanding of how through Christ we sinners are made pleasing to God—Luther's theology of baptism makes little sense, just as apart from baptism, his doctrine of justification remains abstract and without much relevance on a personal level.

Apart from the specific texts addressing baptism, we can consider as foundational the texts where Luther first formulated his distinctive theology about the devastating human condition and God's undeserved promise of restoration through the person and work of Christ. Long before writing the Catechisms or explicit texts on baptism, Luther made important arguments pertaining to baptism in his first lectures on the Bible, namely on the Psalms (1513–1515), Hebrews (1517) and, especially, Romans (1515–1516) and Galatians (1516–1517), his very favorite epistles. When explaining the gift of justification in these texts, he laid the foundation for how to consider baptism.

Similarly in his *Heidelberg Disputation* from 1518, Luther's radical vision about how we may expect to know the hidden God as one revealed to us in Christ's suffering was as important to his theology of baptism as his conclusion that human beings become pleasing to God only because of God's descending, creative love. One of Luther's most disturbing conclusions was: "[One] who does not know Christ does not know God hidden in suffering. . . . God can be found only in suffering and the cross."[1] In this treatise Luther set an expectation for the life of the baptized not as a life of glory but that of the cross; that is, Christian life is not an apparent success story. It is never free from misfortunes, ailments, and ills of many kinds. According to Luther, Christian life is lived in the shadow of an ongoing battle between the draw to good and the draw to the opposite, and God surprises us with God's presence in the lowest points of this existence. To make sense of that is to make sense of the cross, and thus to do the work of a true theologian. In this light, we can presuppose with Luther that as baptized persons we are all theologians, engaged in life and making sense of it.

Another important work in this regard is Luther's *On Christian Freedom* (1520), a widely read treatise that has spoken to people through the generations. This treatise is relevant for Luther's theology of baptism, for in it he described the mode of Christian life and spirituality for those baptized in the name of Christ, doing it in a way that spoke to real people and inspired them to think theologically about their lives. In this work Luther proclaimed the wild thought that, because of Christ, we are free from all that binds us the "wrong" way and are liberated and bound in a "good" way to others, because of love for God and love for one another. Seeking the meaning of that freedom and bondage "for me," in "my life," is at the heart of intentional spiritual living, that is, spirituality. It is what life as a baptized Christian is all about.

Other treatises from 1520, the fateful year when Luther laid out his "reformation visions" and alienated himself from the Catholic Church, are important for his views on baptism as well. In particular, in the *Babylonian Captivity of the Church* he challenged the very basics of the church's teaching of the sacraments and redefined their meaning and use to benefit the people needing them spiritually rather than those concerned about bringing in money for the church or using the sacraments for control. He wished to liberate the sacraments from what he considered wrong in their use and instruction about them, and he did so with a renewed emphasis on their gift-nature. What Luther said in his

1520 treatises about grace, freedom, and responsibilities of Christian life, formed a basis for how he would teach about baptism to people who had questions about their faith and "fate," about their relationship with God and one another, and about their belonging to the church and status as Christians. When teaching baptism, Luther taught about "everything" that mattered, spiritually speaking. Luther concluded in the *Babylonian Captivity of the Church* that baptism signified two things—death and resurrection—that is, full and complete justification. These words are indicative: in baptism we are dealing with everything from birth to death and beyond.

From this quick look at some of the key writings of Luther we can see how baptism was central to his teaching about justification. When seeking a gracious God who finds human beings pleasing, when imagining ways through which human beings become filled with God's grace and are spiritually transformed, when envisioning the direction and possibilities for the resulting Christian life for those justified—that is, restored in a personal, forgiven relationship with God, and renewed in Christ—Luther cast his eyes on baptism as the touch point. It is in baptism that all this becomes personally meaningful. If in all theology and religious practices the ultimate goal is to know God and experience God's presence in our lives, then baptism should be at the center of our attention. Why so? Because, according to Luther, in that holy act God becomes ours.

A Matter of Respectful Reverence

Out of his respect for God the Almighty, Luther was quite exercised over the need to approach baptism with an attitude of reverence and appreciation. In his 1523 *Baptismal Booklet* Luther wrote, "Out of a sense of Christian commitment, I appeal to all those who baptize, sponsor infants, or witness a baptism to take to heart the tremendous work and great solemnity present here." He spoke of the holiness of the ritual: "For here in the words of these prayers you hear how plaintively and earnestly the Christian church brings the infant to God, confesses before him with such unchanging, undoubting words that the infant is possessed by the devil and a child of sin and wrath, and so diligently asks for help and grace through baptism, that the infant may become a child of God."[2]

Important confessions of faith are made when we baptize or even simply participate in baptism. First, we acknowledge the existence and presence of evil and sin. Second, we launch a deliberate attempt to face and conquer that reality. Third, we trust that the baptized enters into personal communion with God and into God's protection. Serious matters indeed! Given the gravity of the premise, Luther reminded readers, there was nothing casual about baptism. All participants needed to approach the act with utmost reverence and decency. (No "drunk" and "boorish" priests or good-for-nothing godparents were to be tolerated!) He strongly admonished all participating in the ritual: "Thus it is extremely necessary to stand by the poor child with all your heart and with a strong faith and plead with great devotion that God, in accordance with these prayers, would not only free the child from the devil's power but also strengthen the child, so that the child might resist him [it] valiantly in life and in death. I fear that people turn out so badly after baptism because we have dealt with them in such a cold and casual way and prayed for them at their baptism without any zeal at all."[3]

Respecting the ritual and taking it seriously goes hand in hand with having faith in its benefits. When we baptize, we express our belief in particular things and we need to believe what we do, Luther insisted. If we do not believe in the need to renounce the devil and be forgiven, if we do not believe in the Holy Spirit and one Christian church, if we do not believe in the resurrection of the body and the community of saints in the life to come, then we have no business baptizing in the first place.

A Matter of the Right Rite

In addition to instilling holy reverence for baptism, Luther considered it very important to educate people about the various parts of the baptismal ritual. Understanding the different parts and their purpose enabled believers to embrace for themselves the meaning of the ritual. At the same time he reminded that "the external ceremonies are least important. . . . For certainly a baptism can occur without any of these things."[4] With this he was referring to such traditions as blowing under the eyes, making the sign of cross, putting salt in the mouth and anointing the baptized, using a robe and lighting the candle—all traditional steps in the ritual to which he had been accustomed. Aware of the variance in different local traditions, and eager to draw his readers' attention to what was really important, Luther wrote, "Instead, see to it that you are present there in true faith, that you listen to God's Word, and that you pray along earnestly."[5]

Faith, God's Word, and sincere intention from those present— these were essential for baptism in Luther's view, and they were not tied to any particular formula. With this in mind, he initially proposed relatively few changes to the medieval rite the reformers had adopted from their church of origin. Even in later years he was far from rigid in imagining baptismal rituals for the new churches. According to Luther, "I did not want to make any marked changes in the order of baptism for the time being . . . but I would not mind if it could be improved." Faithful to his own teaching that when introducing changes, one should not burden those weak in faith and with "weak consciences," he saw it wise to proceed slowly when reforming matters dear to people. After all, he concluded, "[h]uman additions do not matter very much, as long as baptism itself is administered with God's word, true faith, and serious prayer."[6]

Looking at the ritual from 1523 that Luther presented as a model, we can conclude that the central parts to him were, on the one hand, those parts that make the ritual a sacrament and as such a truly effective ritual, and, on the other hand, the parts that make it a spiritually meaningful ceremony for the one receiving baptism. The bottom line is that he wished to emphasize above anything else God's action and God's glory in the ritual.

Following the tradition he inherited, Luther considered the use of the ancient trinitarian formula of baptizing in the name of the Father and the Son and the Holy Spirit the most important aspect. This "formula" made the baptism a Christian baptism, for it intentionally invoked God to be present in God's fullness. Given Luther's emphasis on the "Word alone" and his constant creative imagining of the work of the Word, reading the gospel was indispensable. Likewise, baptism as an extension of Christ's ministry naturally had to include remembering him in the texts and praying with him in his own words using the Lord's Prayer. Luther also considered the baptismal vows to be significant because they signaled the beginning of the baptized person's intimate relationship with Christ; the vows made it personal. Dressing the baptized in a white robe as a symbol of the new life and of human nakedness in the eyes of God was fine with Luther—after all, we bring God nothing but an empty slate, thus the color of white was most appropriate! Like Augustine, Luther prioritized exorcism, the ritualized driving out of bad spirits. To him this was of vital importance, as he personally battled what he called the devil all his life. As Lutheranism developed, however, exorcisms were often omitted, whereas other benefits became emphasized instead. Today Lutheran rituals come in both forms: those including parts about purging the "evil" and those omitting them.

As years went by, Luther's theological emphasis in the ritual went through a slight change. Instead of emphasizing full immersion in the water as a sign of death and resurrection with Christ and regeneration with the Spirit—in a ritual where a "generous use of water" was a priority—Luther began to emphasize the effectiveness of God's Word explicitly. In simplifying further what the sacrament was about and for whom it was given, he underscored the centrality of Christ's command and the institution with a promise. He continued to teach that the liturgy was for everybody, including infants, and that it required only two parts to be effective and of value: the coming together of Word and water, after Christ's command (Matthew 28). That, for Luther, defined baptism as a sacrament, a ritual that brings God's grace to us personally.

An issue Luther had to give more attention to was that of faith. He urged people to have faith in the Word and the promise proclaimed as the basis of the ritual. What kind of faith was he talking about? What role does faith have in receiving the benefits of baptism? Given that Luther's most famous theological argument was that human beings are saved and justified by grace through faith, it is not surprising that faith would surface as a central issue for him to continue to elaborate on, also in terms of baptism.

The Rite of Baptism Today

Both the rite Luther inherited and the one he passed on were significantly longer and more elaborate than our modern Lutheran liturgies, but Lutheran baptisms taking place today in North American and European settings certainly include the elements that Luther considered essential. Water is always used and the Word is proclaimed as the person is baptized. We continue to baptize in the name of the Triune God, and in that we continue to baptize specifically in the name of Jesus and into the company of Jesus, with the hope and promise of the baptized person's inclusion in the kingdom of God that Jesus promised and with an invitation to join the work of Jesus toward the kingdom of God here on earth. Some rituals have even reintroduced the aspect of exorcism and liberation from "evil spirits." The baptismal vows typically include the family and congregation bringing the child to baptism and to its membership. The white dress is still often (but not always) used, and candles are lighted and passed on in a family-centered ceremony. Lighting of candles was a trivial, if not a problematic matter for Luther, who wished, if anything, to simplify the ritual to better remind people of what it was about. In today's ceremonies the lighting of a candle enhances the symbolism of the new light the Word and the baptized will bring to the world, and it is found meaningful in the otherwise "wordy" and word-centered ceremony. (It also offers opportunities to include older children or other family members to participate in non-verbal ways.)

We continue the centuries-old tradition of baptism as we continue to share the beliefs of Christians before us. When we receive our baptism, we can record the date and time when we personally joined the tradition and when the beliefs at the heart of it became ours to hold close. When we remember our baptismal day, we can remember actually all the dates when God has become "real" on a personal level to humankind through the ages, and we can anticipate the dates when God's presence comes real in new ways for us all.

For Reflection and Discussion

1. Why is it important to teach the meaning of baptism to others, as well as to seek anew an understanding of the sacrament for ourselves? Why did Luther see it important?

2. What is needed for baptism to be valid? What did Luther say about the actual ritual and what was central in it?

3. What did Luther mean when he talked about the need to approach the ritual with appropriate reverence? How can we show appropriate reverence? What would be the opposite?

4. What can we make of Luther's emphasis on the importance of baptism and of his certainty of the gifts it entails? What shaped his thinking? Are our concerns and experiences similar to his?

5. What difference does it make that Luther tied the meaning of baptism to the "work" of God's Word and God in Three Persons?

3

Baptism as a Sacrament, a Means of Grace

A Holy Sign for the Church to Use

Sacraments in the life of Christian church(es) have been those special concrete acts that are believed to convey grace and a special blessing from God. In the Lutheran church only two such rituals are recognized: baptism and the Lord's Supper. In the Roman Catholic Church, seven rituals are considered sacraments. Other Protestant churches' views on the matter vary. In terms of the roots of the Lutheran conviction, the sixteenth-century reformers were actually less particular about the number and more concerned about the faithfulness with which God's gospel and grace were to be offered to people with the recognizable means available. The reformers stressed the continuity with the apostolic times. It was imperative that the model for the practice was found in Scripture, with an explicit command from Jesus and with a specific promise attached. Nothing new was to be invented in this area.

Luther explained in his *Large Catechism*: "What is baptism? Namely, that it is not simply plain water, but water placed in the setting of God's Word and commandment and made holy by them. It is nothing else than God's water, not that the water itself is nobler than other water but that God's Word and commandment are added to it."[1]

Luther and Lutherans after him found the biblical basis for baptism in Jesus' command in Matthew 28 to go and make all people his disciples, teaching them according to his teachings and baptizing them in the name of the Father and the Son and the Holy Spirit. His promise to accompany this command was: "Remember, I am with you always, to the end of the age" (v. 20). Baptism is a sign of that promise for us to remember, and it is a holy sign for the church to care for.

Luther was a firm believer in the effectiveness of such signs, to be experienced personally. He was also a firm believer in the institutional means of grace, to be used externally. What does all this mean? In short, baptism is a specific means given expressly for the church to use as an external matter and ritual, and in that context it becomes a meaningful holy sign with transformative effects. Baptism has the power to transform our lives and even the world, little by little, through the personal lives that become changed into agents of something incredibly holy as a result of being baptized.

To explain a little further, Luther believed there was need for an organized community of believers—a church—with agreed-upon practices and principles about how to speak the message of gospel to themselves and others and with a shared commitment to offer the means of grace available as prudently and compassionately as possible. He believed that God would work through such an organized community, built around the gospel's proclamation and use of sacraments. God would be at work where people came to hear the Word proclaimed and interpreted to learn and grow, and where people came to sit at the table symbolizing Christian fellowship, to be spiritually energized in the company of other believers and in celebrating the reception of Christ's presence in the wine and the bread. Christian communities have an important place and responsibility in this world to rightfully and efficiently offer and teach the meaning of these holy signs. Without these signs, there would be no church or use for it, and vice versa.

Baptism belongs to the life and use of the church, and Luther's words about it need to be understood in that light. To be sure, only within the church is baptism administered for its original purposes; it is a public Christian occasion in that regard. It should not happen randomly and it should not be used in nonchalant ways but always in earnest and within the church where it belongs as one of its building blocks. It is effective and used right in the context of a Christian community, where the holy sign "means" that for which it was instituted and where people are consciously seeking to unfold its meaning. In other words, outside the Christian church, baptism has little if any meaning, externally speaking. Internally speaking, it is a different matter. And that is another emphasis of Luther: the invisible nature of baptism and what it brings about as an external means of the invisible grace.

Humble Water for Us to "Know"

When gauging baptism as a ritual, Luther advised that we should not look at just what appears to the physical eye but we should look with the spiritual eye at what happens when simple water is joined with the water-changing Word. Of utmost importance is what this mystery means for us, internally and personally; only then can it make a difference outside of us, externally. At the same time, since we are limited in our ability to see and experience fully all that happens in the mysterious act of justification, we have the external ritual of baptism and the memory of it to hold on to, as a fact. According to Luther, "It is of the greatest importance that we regard baptism as excellent, glorious and exalted." This was so regardless of those insisting "that baptism is an external thing and that external things are of no use" and who only see humble water and nothing else.[2]

In Luther's emphasis, the bottom line is God's will and promise: "But no matter how external it may be, here stand God's word and command that have instituted, established, and confirmed baptism. What God institutes and commands cannot be useless. Rather it is a most precious thing, even though to all appearances it may not be worth a straw."[3] Baptism as such may not look that glamorous, but we should know that the plain water becomes most excellent when it becomes a means of God's act.

Water in baptism, as well as grain and grapes in the Lord's Supper (the other Lutheran sacrament), are elements we can feel, taste, see, even digest and thus know through our senses. As such, they assist and support a faith that is not so tangible, not something we can taste, feel, and see, other than its results in our lives—the so-called fruit of faith or the fruit of the Spirit. Faith needs a seed and nurturing and assistance, and the sacrament is for that purpose: to generate appreciation in us toward what God has given for us. From the position of faith, the sacrament becomes alive and meaningful. In Luther's words, "Thus you see plainly that baptism is not a work that we do but that it is a treasure that God gives us and faith grasps, just as the Lord Christ upon the cross is not a work but a treasure placed in the setting of the Word and offered to us in the Word and received by faith." According to Luther, "[I]t is far more glorious than anything else God has commanded and ordained; in short, it is so full of comfort and grace that heaven and earth cannot comprehend it."[4]

Heavenly Water for the Holy Spirit's Landing

Following the reasoning of Augustine, Luther explained the mystery of sacrament from the act of God and God's Word in particular: "For the real significance of the water lies in God's Word or commandment and God's name, and this treasure is greater and nobler than heaven and earth." Baptismal water is different from any other water, not because of "the natural substance but because here something nobler is added, for [God] stakes [God's] honor, power, and might on it."[5]

Baptismal water becomes different as God enters the water, and God does that through the Word—thus the necessity of the Word in the ritual. As a result, "Therefore it is not simply a natural water, but a divine, heavenly, holy and blessed water—praise it in any other terms you can—all by virtue of the Word, which is a heavenly, holy Word that no one can sufficiently extol, for it contains and conveys all that is God's."[6]

That this is now water where God is present and acting is not that apparent to us and our senses. A certain hiddenness remains with baptism and how it conveys God and God's grace. Nonetheless, Luther insisted that what happened to Jesus in his baptism—the Holy Spirit came upon him—is what happens to us, too. Just as the Holy Spirit descended on Jesus, God's Spirit comes to dwell in us. We receive this grace invisibly, but this does not mean that its fruits should remain invisible. Quite the contrary: as God becomes the subject of our lives in baptism and as Christ's heart becomes ours and the Holy Spirit becomes our counselor and guide, how could that not make a difference in our lives? Is it possible that the fruits of lives transformed by such grace could remain hidden?

Baptism Is God's Work

According to Luther, "To be baptized in God's name is to be baptized not by human beings but by God. . . . Although [baptism] is performed by human hands, it is nevertheless truly God's own act."[7] An act of God's Word, to be specific.

Throughout Scripture the Word is the agent and the force that makes things happen. This is particularly true in the case of the sacraments. Just as the Word created the world (Genesis 1) and impregnated young Mary (Luke 1), similarly, it is the Word that comes to water and bread and wine and confers grace to those who come in contact with this powerful mixture. None of this would happen without the Word. For us to receive forgiveness and for the Holy Spirit to work in us, we need the Word—the Word that incorporates all that Christ is and has. According to Luther, "The Holy Spirit must always work in us through the Word, granting us daily forgiveness until we attain to that life where there will be no more forgiveness."[8] Without the Word, "we would have nothing more than a bath-keeper's baptism at our disposal," wrote Luther, using kitchen imagery to illustrate his point: "I therefore admonish you again that these two, the Word and the water must by no means be separated from each other. For where the Word is separated from the water, the water is no different from the water that the maid uses for cooking and could indeed be called a bath-keeper's baptism. But when the Word is with it according to God's ordinance, baptism is a sacrament, and it is called Christ's baptism. This is the first point to be emphasized: the nature and dignity of the holy sacrament."[9] By the same token, when underscoring the "nature and dignity of the holy sacrament," Luther insisted that the Word needed a tangible element, an element that God can make God's own and thereby reach us in a way most fitting to our being.[10]

When referring to the Word, Luther meant not only the written word in Scripture but all that is entailed in the second person of the Trinity. *Word* means Christ's person and all that Christ has done and revealed for us about God. The Word in, from, about, and because of Christ's person and life is how we can know God—scandalously and surprisingly so. The Word is the divine agent through which God approaches humanity before, in, and after the incarnation of Christ. This Word is spiritual and comes to us spiritually, just as God is spiritual. At the same time, the Word becomes tangible when bound to matter, just as Christ's divinity is bound to humanity—a real flesh and blood human being who cried a newborn's cry at birth and who cried a dying man's wail at the cross.

So when Luther underscored the effectiveness of the Word, he was underscoring the sole activity of God in the acts of grace. When emphasizing the role of Christ and the need for a material to accompany the Word, he was emphasizing the reality of the divine presence that encompasses all human life and experience. Both claims are at the heart of how Luther understood the way our personal relationship with God is possible at all.

In Luther's emphasis, then, baptism has two dimensions we need to keep in mind: the invisible spiritual and the visible material. Both are needed in order for God to meet us in our spiritual and physical ways of being. Luther's words sum it up: "This is the reason why these two things are done in baptism; the body has water poured over it, because all it can receive is the water, and in addition the Word is spoken so that the soul may receive it. Because the water and the Word together constitute one baptism, both body and soul shall be saved and live forever: the soul through the Word in which it believes, the body because it is united with the soul and apprehends baptism in the only way it can."[11]

To return to the child's question posed earlier—whether we should remember our baptismal date—in light of what we think of a sacrament, we could yelp with Luther a firm yes! That is the date when we get to "know" God in our senses and in our hearts, before we understand anything with our heads. The date reminds us of when and where we were personally offered a drowning dose of grace and received its very real benefits. The date reminds us to be grateful that people acted on our behalf, wrapping us in grace for which we could not even imagine to ask. The date reminds us of the faith of the community of believers who trusted in the power and meaning of the ritual "for me" and performed the ritual, hooking us in the old tradition of believing how God has come to us in flesh and continues to come to us in Word and water. The date also reminds us of our entrance to the community of believers with full rights and privileges, as well as new responsibilities. The date reminds us of what we have received; it also reminds us of what God has promised to *all* humankind, not just us—grace.

For Reflection and Discussion

1. How would you explain sacrament to a seven-year-old child who just "baptized" a kitten?

2. Why is water important in baptism? Why is Word important in baptism? What else is important for baptism to be more than a sacred ritual?

3. What does our belief in sacraments tell us about what we believe about God and God's grace?

4. What role does faith play in baptism and in our lives as baptized followers of Jesus?

4

Baptism as Justification

Baptism as Union with Christ

Luther's most famous and influential theological insight was that human beings are made right with God and become pleasing to God only by faith. Luther called this justification by faith. However, lest we think such faith is of our own doing, Luther repeated time and again that this is a matter of grace.

Justification—being put right with God—is a gift, and it is so because of what Christ has done and who Christ is. This is the heart of Luther's theology, and it is in this light that we can appreciate baptism in all its promise. Baptism brings the idea of justification home on a personal level. In his 1518 *Heidelberg Disputation*, Luther explained justification in a rich and provocative way: "the love of God which lives in [human beings] loves sinners, evil persons, fools, and weaklings in order to make them righteous, good, wise, and strong. Rather than seeking its own good, the love of God flows forth and bestows good. Therefore sinners are attractive because they are loved; they are not loved because they are attractive."[1]

Luther often used two words to describe justification and its source and effects—*alien* and *righteousness*: "There are two kinds of Christian righteousness. . . . The first is alien righteousness, that is the righteousness of another, instilled from without. This is the righteousness of Christ by which he justifies through faith."[2] Luther taught that there is no such righteousness or goodness inborn or growing independently in us, and there is no such righteousness or goodness or blessedness that we can bring about by our own effort that could make God love us. The source of such goodness and loveliness and beauty is outside of us—in Christ. In addition to this alien righteousness, Luther does talk about "our own," "proper" righteousness, but that always follows the first kind.

At the heart of how Luther explained justification by grace through faith is his conviction that Christ becomes ours and gives us all that is his. This becomes personally meaningful for us in baptism. In that wash we become as attractive to God as Christ is because all God sees when looking at us is Christ. How does that happen? In the act of baptism, by the power of the Word and the water, Christ in God's fullness enters our very being. Luther called this a "happy exchange"—when Christ receives our humanness and sins and when we receive Christ's love and goodness.[3] "Through faith in Christ, therefore, Christ's righteousness becomes our righteousness and all that he has becomes ours; rather, he himself becomes ours."[4] We can "with confidence boast in Christ and say: 'Mine are Christ's living, doing, and speaking, his suffering and dying, mine as much as if I had lived, done, spoken, suffered, and died as he did.'"[5] Indeed, as the words of our baptismal ritual proclaim, we "have been sealed by the Holy Spirit and marked with the cross of Christ forever."[6]

Baptism as Transformation

Luther's explanation of how we are made right with God in union with Christ is very rich, even mystical, in the way that Luther described invisible, godly "things" and the realm of being that defies scientific measure but that can be appreciated through faith. Luther's words resonate with those of the Christian mystics before and after him who sought personal closeness to God and spoke of their experienced union with God and the humbling transformation that unfolded from that journey.[7] Where Luther differed from the mystics of his time, however, was in his conviction that this union is not something we can ever find by ourselves or even desire to seek, but it is simply given to us, without special pre-requisites or merits. As baptized, we all can rejoice with Luther in the confidence that we have been granted "very great and precious gifts in Christ." The gift of Christ given in baptism makes us stand on par with the great mystics of the church and the saints who have sought to know God on a personal, intimate level. We can be bold to rejoice that we are in a "knowing union" with God, because God has come to us. This is what takes place in justification; this is what takes place in baptism.[8]

Lutherans after Luther's time have overlooked an important emphasis in his teaching about justification and baptism—the importance he placed on the real change or transformation that occurs in our being because of Jesus. We are accustomed to talking about forgiveness given in baptism, and we are used to describing justification as an act of being pronounced "not guilty" because of what Christ has done. Luther, however, invited his readers to consider: How does becoming one with God transform us? How does baptism change our lives?

In Luther's view, we change *internally*, and that change should show *externally*. Just as our status in relation to God changes when Christ actually enters our lives, so our responsibilities in the world change. As justified, baptized persons, we live with new responsibilities and possibilities in our relationships, divine and human. Just as a wedding is not the end of a love relationship but rather the beginning of life together, baptism is not an end in itself either. Baptism is the beginning of our life in a personal covenant and union with God our Creator, Redeemer, and Sustainer. The life that ensues is not just any kind of life but godly life, Christ-filled life.

Baptism as Beginning of Servanthood

Baptism is a springboard for godly living in this world. Luther called this "our own righteousness," and he was quick to point out that this "second kind of righteousness" always followed "Christ's righteousness." (As in, gifts first, then expressions of gratitude! Or, perhaps, plug in to the power and the motor will run.) Luther was not talking about chronology but causality. His main point was that we cannot live a godly life without Christ; we cannot grow in our own righteousness without the gift righteousness of Christ. That said, all the grace given to us in baptism and in the person of Christ should make us conscious of the call to live as Christs to one another.

The two dimensions of righteousness—alien and proper—illuminate how we can understand the effects of baptism, first in terms of our wellbeing in the company of the divine, and second, in this world in the company of the other "creatures." According to Luther, we first receive the gift of a new start, with forgiveness and freedom from things that bind. This freedom is akin to the feeling that follows the lifting of guilt for something terrible we have done, or the release that comes when hearing good news of healing from serious illness, or the feeling of parents or spouses who regret things said and done in daily frustration and are grateful for each new day they can start with a clean slate. Throughout our lives, we need and receive many such new beginnings. Not to worry, Luther concluded, this is exactly what is granted in baptism: the gift of forgiveness and new beginning, renewed every time we return to it, every time we repent and remember why we need baptism in the first place, every time we realize we need God to help guide and sustain us. Usually when we do that, we feel sorry for ourselves and experience shame and regret. That is not all bad, as long as we remember, as Luther reminded, that, "Repentance, therefore, is nothing else than a return and approach to baptism, to resume and practice what has earlier been begun but abandoned."[9]

Baptism and repentance together are for us to use and draw from on a daily basis. In fact, Luther described Christian life specifically as "nothing else than a daily baptism, begun once and continuing even after. For we must keep at it without ceasing, always purging whatever pertains to the old Adam, so that whatever belongs to the new creature may come forth."[10] Seeking a helpful image, Luther urged, "Therefore let all Christians regard their baptism as the daily garment that they are to wear all the time. Every day they should be found in faith and with its fruits, suppressing the old creature and growing up in the new."[11] We may have a hard time relating to Luther's image of "suppressing the old creature," but on a gut level we know what he was talking about—us in our humanness, warts and all. We can find quite appealing his idea of a heavenly "garment."

The garment offered in baptism comes in handy. Our life is a battle. We live in the tension between "fully healed and holy" and "yet not";

full of God's presence and blessings, yet unable to make the most of it. We live lives full of complex relations where we hurt and get hurt. We hear and cause bad news every day. We fight, we lie, we cheat, we are shallow and selfish. We tend to forget God, not to mention the well-being of our neighbor. We lose sight of the glimpses of God given to us in the different moments of each day. We get distracted and become self-absorbed. The list goes on and on.

As much as Luther emphasized the completeness of justification—our complete restoration in relationship to God and the Spirit-induced transformation that takes place in baptism specifically—he also envisioned justification as something lived here and now as a progress we are engaged in throughout our lives. This "other" kind of righteousness—"our own"—is like a leavening process, the yeast eventually permeating every inch of the dough, fermenting it and causing it to rise, until it bubbles out of the bowl.

If baptism is the starting point of our new life in Christ, what then is the goal? What ultimately is the result of a baptism-fermented life? What is the leavening about? About reaching perfection and being spiritually superior to others? No, not that. Luther's vision was not about comparisons or qualitative, measured progress of personal gain or spiritual improvement. We do not measure "better" or "worse" in this life. We do not "grow" to be essentially "better." We are who we are. At the same time, we can make a difference in the way we relate to others and how we treat life around us. One way to look at the irresistible power of baptism-induced fermenting in us is to see it as expanding our hearts to embrace the concerns of others. Like really yeasty dough, God's love stirs and fills our life to the point that it cannot possibly be contained in a single bowl; it needs to expand. So the goal is not solely our own spiritual wellbeing but rather the spiritual and material wellbeing of others: justification brings us to a right relationship with God and stirs us to love and serve the other. In Luther's words, "this righteousness consists in love to one's neighbor."[12]

There we have it. All the gifts given to us—justification and forgiveness, righteousness and union with God (that is, restored relationship with our Creator and a personal union with Christ the

Savior)—are actually ours for the benefit of others as much as for the benefit of ourselves. Love and service of the other are the operative words for our life as members of Christ's church who believe that we are made right with God in the act of baptism. Christ's altruistic life is the model given to us who believe we are made one with him in our baptism. Baptism is the starting point in a love relationship with God and one another. It is about starting our lives anew, with second chances, because of Christ's love for us. And it is about us living as Christ for one another and serving one another in love, because God has loved and served us first.

These are the reasons why we baptize: we baptize because we want to live like Christ and invite others to live that way too, and we baptize because we believe it is possible and necessary. In Luther's words, "If we want to be Christians, we must practice the work that makes us Christians, and let those who fall away return to it."[13] What makes us Christians is Christ. We are named after the one in whose name we are baptized for a reason: "Surely we are named after Christ, not because he is absent from us, but because he dwells in us, that is, because we believe in him and are Christs to one another and do to our neighbor as Christ does to us."[14] This indeed is the whole point of being a Christian and being justified and baptized: servanthood and love. Being Christian means living a life founded on and guided by love, the love of Christ specifically, received and given, because of what Christ has done in godly love.

The model given to us is impossible if left up to us alone, but is possible because of the gift given to us for this purpose exactly, a gift that is ours to unwrap again and again as often as we need to. The main reason for unwrapping the gift is not our own pleasure and gain, but how "what we've got" empowers us to live and love as Christ did. Luther wrote: "'Let this mind be in you, which was also in Christ Jesus' [Phil. 2:5]. This means you should be as inclined and disposed towards one another as you see Christ was disposed toward you."[15] For Luther, taking on Christ in the form of a servant is the mode of a baptized person: "We conclude, therefore, that a Christian lives not in himself [or herself], but in Christ and in his neighbor. Otherwise he is not a

Christian. He lives in Christ through faith, in his neighbor through love. By faith he is caught up beyond himself into God. By love he descends beneath himself into his neighbor."[16]

Born Again in Baptism?

Lutherans do not generally use "born-again" language, but in light of what Luther believed about justification, these words certainly could belong in our vocabulary, particularly when talking about the *effects* of baptism. Such effects are described beautifully in this baptismal prayer offered during Luther's time: "The almighty God and Father of our Lord Jesus Christ, who has given birth to you for a second time through water and the Holy Spirit and has forgiven you all your sins, strengthen you with his grace to eternal life. Amen."[17]

Birth for the second time is exactly what happens in baptism. What is amazing, though, is while this rebirth is at once complete, it is also experienced on an ongoing basis throughout our lives. It is "once and for all," but its effects are life-renewing each and every day. Each time we remember our baptism and the reason for which it is given, it is as if we relive or actualize our rebirth; our consciousness of it makes it come alive for us.

We could ask, what role, if any, does faith play in our being "born again"? This question is particularly relevant in light of the different Christian teachings about being reborn, especially from those denominations where much emphasis is put on charistmatic "born-again" experiences. Luther made it clear that baptism grants the new birth by the mere act performed in the community of believers. It is valid as such, but without faith baptism would never mean to us what it is supposed to mean. Faith makes baptism more than an empty symbol; it causes us to believe in the full meaning of baptism and its real effects for us.[18] As Luther wrote: "Just by allowing the water to be poured over you, you do not receive or retain baptism in such a manner that it does you any good. But it becomes beneficial to you if you accept it as God's command and ordinance, so that, baptized in God's name, you may receive in the water the promised salvation. Neither the hand nor the body can do this, but rather the heart must believe it."[19]

Though Luther seemed aware of the difficulty of believing in a second, spiritual kind of birth, by using birth imagery he tried to bring home the amazing mystery involved in the event. Anybody who has witnessed or gone through pregnancy and childbirth is prone to be in awe of how is it possible that a tiny seed grows into a human being in such a confined place and manages to emerge alive and breathe on his or her own. We believe that it is possible when we see it happen, yet we cannot ultimately explain it or make it happen. We are just grateful that it does happen and that it happened to us. Life is real and tangible, and at the same time, life is miraculous and beyond our grasp; we are humbled to be part of it. The same is true in regard to our spiritual, second birth; in faith we can be sure that it does happen and that it happens to us. We cannot make it happen, but the giver of life can, and does so whether we believe it or not. It comes to mean something to us once we begin to believe it as true and important "for me," once we have faith.

When Luther wrote, "The one who believes and is baptized will be saved," he meant to underscore how both faith and baptism save. Blessings offered in the water and in the Word are to be believed from the heart. Otherwise, "Without faith baptism is of no use, although in itself it is an infinite, divine treasure."[20] This does not mean, however, that our baptism and its effectiveness in any way would depend on us or on a special kind of faith we somehow produce. Yet, he does point out faith as the agent, so to speak, in our being made right with God and in baptism becoming meaningful and transforming in our lives. But Luther had a particular faith in mind here, one that comes from God: "Faith is not the human notion and dream that some people call faith." Instead, "[f]aith . . . is a divine work in us which changes us and makes us to be born anew of God, John 1[:12-13]. It kills the old Adam and makes us altogether different men [people], in heart and spirit and mind and powers; and it brings with it the Holy Spirit."[21] This kind of faith changes us, and brings us closer to God. We need both baptism—a concrete act—and faith—the very means that open the spiritual dimension for us. Together they make Christ's promise real for us, manifesting in us the "fruits" of God's love: "Therefore, if we recognize the great and precious things which are given us, as Paul says [Rom. 5:5], our hearts will be filled by the Holy Spirit with the love which makes us free, joyful, almighty workers and conquerors over all tribulations, servants of our neighbors, and yet lords of all."[22]

Lutherans with Luther can talk about "born-again" experiences, as long as we keep the emphasis on God as the source of that experience and servanthood as its ongoing result. We can believe that baptism effects a change in us and we can believe in the saving power of faith, both occurring in baptism, both given to us. Unlike those denominations that tend to tie the experience of renewal to evidence of a person's spiritual development or special encounter of faith, Lutherans with Luther can appreciate the ongoing effect of the sacrament as an external God-given means of grace at the root of faith-based spiritual living.

For Reflection and Discussion

1. What does it mean that baptism makes us attractive to God? Does it make us more lovable and loving to one another as well?

2. What does it mean that we receive in baptism Christ, the Holy Spirit, and full God in Three Persons? How does this happen? Can we feel this? Does it show?

3. Can Lutherans talk about "born-again" experience and "rebirth"? How so? How does our understanding differ from that of other denominations and religions?

4. Holiness in servanthood—what kind of a starting point is that for a life of the baptized?

5

Baptism as the Greatest Comfort

Is Baptism Necessary for Salvation?

Lutherans for centuries have proclaimed that baptism is necessary for salvation. The stimulus for this comes from Luther, but also from the central Lutheran confessional text, *The Augsburg Confession* (1530), where a Lutheran position on baptism and its necessity is articulated.[1] There are two versions of the confession, one in German and one in Latin, and they actually phrase the necessity of baptism slightly differently.[2]

The German version of the document states that, "Concerning baptism it is taught that it is necessary, that grace is offered through it, and that one should also baptize children, who through such baptism are entrusted to God and become pleasing to him."[3] The Latin text says, "Concerning baptism they teach that it is necessary for salvation, that the grace of God is offered through baptism, and that children should be baptized. They are received into the grace of God when they are offered to God though baptism."[4]

Looking at the slightly different wordings, we could conclude that the texts are mutually conflicting and that the sixteenth-century writers were not clear or in agreement with what to say about the matter. Or we can conclude that the words need to be read in a broader light and that the word *necessary* has many meanings, all of which negate seeing baptism as some sort of safety net or magical protective act and ticket to salvation. If the texts are interpreted in light of one another, we can actually conclude that the word *necessary* refers to the strongly articulated call of the church to go and preach and teach and offer God's grace through this certain means. This act is necessary for the mission of the church, just as grace itself is necessary for each of us. Baptism is necessary for these reasons and only in this light, but not as itself.

Regardless of how the word *necessary* has been understood, Lutherans have continued to baptize infants as well as adults, holding on to the immeasurable promises of life-giving and life-sustaining grace, full forgiveness of all that separates us from God, inconceivable and unmerited redemption from guilt, and a radical deliverance to a new life with God and one another. Without these gifts, how could we survive, spiritually speaking? How could we live a spiritually meaningful life? How could we hope for life to conquer death? Can we imagine our lives without grace, and thus without God? Here is the basis for the necessity we talk about regarding baptism: we need grace just as we need air to breathe; we need God in order to live. Baptism is about us as a community of believers recognizing this necessity and acting upon it for the sake of us all. And act we must, because of another "necessity" that has come into human life, and that is sin.

Enslaved to Sin

At the root of our Lutheran beliefs concerning sacraments in general and baptism in particular are certain assumptions about our human nature and the Divinity. What are the premises of the relationship between human beings and God, and what are the possible obstacles? We acknowledge that human life involves sin in its many forms, in all the negativity that threatens to separate us from God and from one another and that causes hurt in our relations in all directions.

Luther's teaching on the matter of devastatingly limited human freedom is crystallized in what he wrote in his *Smalcald Articles*: "Here we must confess (as St. Paul says [in] I Rom. 5[:12]) that sin comes from that one human being, Adam, through whose obedience all people became sinners and subject to death and the devil. This is called the original sin, or the chief sin. This is the beginning and the root of sin that manifests in so many different ways. The fruits of this sin are the subsequent evil words, which are forbidden in the Ten Commandments, such as unbelief, false belief, idolatry, being without the fear of God, presumption, despair, blindness, and, in short, not knowing or honoring God. Beyond that, there is lying, swearing [falsely] by God's name, not praying or calling on God's name, neglect of God's Word, being disobedient to parents, murdering, behaving promiscuously, stealing, deceiving, etc." According to Luther, this damage is bigger and graver than we can understand. "This inherited sin has caused such a deep, evil corruption of nature that reason does not comprehend it; rather it must be believed on the basis of the revelation in the Scriptures (Ps. 51[:5] and Rom. 5[:12], Exod. 33[:20]; Gen. 3[:6ff.])."[5]

Luther argued that because of the first sin of disobedience, human beings are in bondage to sin and are not free to love God or make right choices in the eyes of God. Because of sin our choices are fallible and our lives mortal. Here Luther offered a striking departure from centuries of Christian teaching that the choice to love God and neighbor is ours to make and that we have the freedom to make that choice.

In *The Bondage of the Will* Luther wrote, with fire, that it is more than evident that "free choice is a pure fiction."[6] Quite the contrary is the reality: all people are simply "ungodly and wicked."[7] All people are "devoid of the knowledge of God and full of contempt for" God; all people, in full person, are simply "lost" and "worthless as regards the good." Luther taught that the human condition is so pitiable that when God looks down from heaven, God sees nobody who would be looking for or minding God, but rather "they all turn aside." The created full freedom is gone; our ability on our own to love God and one another—or even ourselves—as God would want is gone. However, love of God for us is not gone. Baptism is the reminder of that and a holy sign as such.

Since we do not have what it takes to free ourselves from all that binds, our only chances are in what God makes happen for us, and baptism is one of those chances. In that regard, it is a must, a necessity we would be fools not to grab on to. Countering arguments to the contrary, Luther admonished, "Ah, dear Christians, let us not value or treat this unspeakable gift so half-heartedly. For baptism is our only comfort and the doorway to all of God's possessions and to the communion of all the saints. To this end may God help us."[8] Indeed, we need God's help to instill faith in us, which is the key that opens the door to a conscious connection to God's realm and to God's protection and makes baptism meaningful for us personally. Such faith, Luther reminded, "is a divine work in us which changes us and makes us to be born anew of God."[9] This new birth is very much like our biological birth: it happens by forces beyond our control; we have very little to do with how it all works out. Baptism, and with it, justification, is a gift, very much like life itself is.

Benefits of Baptism

There are certain benefits in baptism that can be highlighted as "musts" in how we understand the presence of sin in our lives and in the world. These benefits can be summarized as: bringing about salvation, bringing about personal union with God, bringing about forgiveness, and bringing about new life with a shield and a booster to accompany us.

Salvation and Union with God

The most important benefit is salvation. According to Luther, "This is the simplest way to put it: the power, effect, benefit, fruit, and purpose of baptism is that it saves. . . . To be saved, as everyone well knows, is nothing else than to be delivered from sin, death, and the devil, to enter into Christ's kingdom, and to live with him forever."[10]

Baptism saves because it returns us to the kind of relationship with God that the Creator had in mind in the first place. God created us to be with God, thus to "redeem us and make us holy" is in line with the Creator's original will, according to which God has in baptism "granted and bestowed upon us everything in heaven and on earth." Everything. Most importantly, God has granted us God's only Child—Christ—and God's own Spirit, through whom God continues to draw us to the Triune God.[11] What more could we hope for?

We would not even dare to hope this, actually. God's own will is the reason that all this happens. This will, Luther suggested, can be understood in light of the commandments and promises given to us in Scripture. The Creeds in particular can be read as explanation of what God gives to us, just as the commandments articulate what God wants from us who are made in God's image and are in covenant with God. When we perform baptism, we are responding to God's commands and promises and acting upon the Creator's own intents. As an act of obedience, in baptism we confess and affirm our belief in God

Baptism brings God to us. When baptizing in the name of the Triune God, we call upon God to be present in this act provided for our benefit. We invite God to come and live in us. But baptism is God's doing, so, more importantly, God invites Godself to live in us and draw us close in a divine love that made us, saved us, and enables us to believe and trust that that love will never end. "Hence the creed can be condensed to these few words," wrote Luther: "'I believe in God the Father, who created me; I believe in God the Son, who has redeemed me; I believe in the Holy Spirit, who makes me holy.'"[12] All this we believe in baptism. Of this we become participants in baptism where God is not only present but acting as the subject, and becoming the subject of our lives radically changed after the ritual set for our benefit.[13]

Forgiveness

Where the effect of baptism becomes most personal is in the act of forgiveness that takes place. In baptism God washes us, lovingly scrubbing away the dirt and filth of sin that clings so closely. Receiving a bath is very intimate; we would not allow just anybody to scrub our backs, just as we would hesitate to give a bath to a stranger. And speaking of strangers, we could think of ourselves as strangers to God, as strangers on the street whom God plucks from the gutter and cleans up, welcomes to a feast table, and gives reason to move on. This kind of radical compassion, closeness, and peculiar acquaintance is at stake with baptism.

Luther reminded his readers that this washing is not accomplished by something special added to the water. Baptism is not a magical act with magical ingredients or super soap. Not even the power of the Word alone makes things happen. Rather, "this washing takes place only through God's will and not at all through the Word and the water."[14] It is God's desire and God's action that accomplishes the "washing of regeneration" that St. Paul talks about in his letter to Titus (3:5).[15]

God forgives us as God washes us, and in so doing, makes it possible for us to forgive others and even ourselves. How important is this washing? To answer that, we need only remember how impossible any relationship is without forgiveness. Baptism as forgiveness, is, among other things, about de-cluttering and wiping away the film of "gunk" and setting aside the baggage that binds us in our relationships and clouds our view of who we are. It purges us inside and out on a level of which we are not even aware.

New Life

Baptism is in effect an entrance into new life with a change in our relationship to God, a change in our being and in how we look to God, and a change in terms of what "lives" in us and guides us. In baptism we are "born of water and Spirit" (John 3:5). We are reminded by Luther that it is in baptism, "through which we, being freed from the devil's tyranny and loosed from sin, death, and hell, become children of life, heirs of all God's possessions, God's own children, and brothers and sisters of Christ."[16] As a result of baptism, God lives in us—Jesus lives in us. As a result of baptism, God's Spirit dwells in us, and God guides and moves and fortifies us. That is why and how baptism provides the protection we need to battle the "enemies" to our well-being and our faith.

Luther's words need to be understood in light of the world in which he lived, a scary world where disease, wars, and tragedies of many kinds brought people to despair and made them weary of death. Within this context, Luther emphasized the seriousness of the matter, teaching first that in baptism we receive medicine and protection. Second, with the baptismal ritual we launch warfare against the "devil" and all the "evils" in the world as we harness the baptized with Christ. The words *evil* and *devil* beg for an explanation for modern readers. Suffice it to say that without necessarily sharing Luther's medieval view of the personified presence of evil, we can relate to his words with our experiences of what we recognize as opposite of good and with our encounters with suffering and destruction and different forms of injustice.

In baptism, Luther promised, we take action against all that stands in enmity toward God and goodness. Baptism is thus to be approached and appreciated with appropriate reverence. It should also give us confidence, trust, and hope. "Thus, we must regard baptism and put it to use in such a way that we may draw strength and comfort from it when our sins or conscience oppress us, and say: 'But I am baptized! And if I have been baptized, I have the promise that I shall be saved and have eternal life, both in soul and body.'"[17]

The Only and All of Baptism

Based on Luther's explanation of the benefits of the sacrament of baptism and our need for it, we can make several important conclusions whether baptism is an inclusive or exclusive means of grace. In Luther's view, the prevalence of sin, the bondage of the will that limits our ability to make right choices and keeps us from loving God and one another as we should, was enough to convince him that spiritually speaking, baptism is "our only comfort and the doorway to all of God's possessions and to the communion of all the saints."[18]

What is his point? Whereas Luther did say baptism was our only comfort, he did not say that baptism was God's only way to us. Luther appeared to mean that of all the rituals for human beings, baptism is the exclusively effective way on which we can boldly rely, primarily because its effectiveness does not depend on us in any way. As such it is a "must" for us to use, and we can be sure of its importance and effectiveness. That said, the word *only* does not need to apply to God and God's options. *Only* is a human concept and applicable in a human world, whereas God is infinite and a God of possibilities beyond human vision. Luther himself might not have been quite this generous in his conclusions, given the more limited worldview and religious framework in which he operated, but his own words give us the stimulus to find quite an inclusive interpretation within the framework of our world.

The word *only* in human language refers to the necessities having to do with the limitations on our end. Evil needs to be exorcised and room needs to be made for the Spirit—that is the premise of Christian baptism. To our knowledge and the conviction of Christians who have gone before us, and based on Scripture, baptism effects all this. Specific parts in the ritual describe how we depart from the devil and the "nasty" and make room for the Spirit and the "good." Lutherans believe that what is described and invoked in baptism truly happens.[19] Baptism in this regard is indeed our sure comfort, as we would be able to achieve none of this on our own. The gifts baptism confers on us do not depend and cannot depend on anything in us but are solely based on God's voluntary act of grace. We desperately need what baptism has to offer, and everything that baptism promises needs to come from God. Thus, God is a "must" for us, as our Creator, Redeemer, and Sanctifier. So it is that we can understand baptism as *our only comfort*.

But what conclusions can we draw about the extensiveness of grace offered in baptism and from Luther's commendation of baptism as "the doorway to all of God's possessions and to the communion of all the saints"?[20] Here lies a powerful promise: in baptism God has arranged a way for us to have not *partial* access to some of God but full access to *all* that is God's. God of lavish grace and extravagant love holds nothing back from the children God names and claims in baptism.

The words *only* and *all* then can be understood as Luther's emphasis on what is essential in baptism: human beings are made right with God and pleasing to God by God's action alone. God has bound God's promise in God's own Word on this particular ritual for our benefit. Another way to say this is that our only comfort and doorway to God is God the Spirit, God of grace who has bound a divine promise in this concrete matter and act. This God comes to be ours—mine—because of Jesus.

Baptism is a unique doorway pointing to a new reality. It is in the rite of baptism that we go through a purification—symbolically and actually—and enter a new relationship with God. We are embraced in a new reality where we are filled with God the Spirit and receive all that Christ has. In baptism we really become children of God; we become one with Christ, God's own child. We know of no other sure way to this relationship in our Christian worldview and tradition. This does not mean there are no other ways, but for us, this is it, and it is worth taking a tight hold of.

Are these good enough reasons to remember our baptismal date? With Luther we can answer yes, as long as it does not imply that those without such a personal date are somehow beyond and without God's merciful ways and design. Our baptismal date reminds us of the certainty of the reality of God coming into our personal lives in Christ. It reminds us of our own fallibility and constant need for God; it reminds us of what Christ has done and continues to do in us and for us and with us. Remembering our baptismal date is a form of confessing our continual need for God's grace. It does not point to the exclusion of those not baptized, but rather the inclusion of us all who are invited by God into God's grace for a life as God's children, after the model of Christ, the "first" child of God.

Baptism reminds us of who God is for us: our Creator who gave and continues to give us life, our Redeemer who cleanses us from our sin and gives us new life again and again, and the Spirit who sustains us and keeps us connected to God. We grow in holiness that is not ours but becomes ours, because God wills it so. Remembering the date of our baptism reminds us of the holiness given for us and for the benefit of the whole world and recalls the amazing ways God comes to this world to be known by us. The date is a proof for us—"for me"—that enforces our faith, so that we can continue to seek the ways and the will of God and demonstrate it in our lives through our own words and our actions.

For Reflection and Discussion

1. How can we understand baptism as "necessary" and yet not the "only" means of salvation and God's grace?

2. What is baptism a "doorway" to? Does "no baptism" mean "door closed"?

3. What kind of a shield and protection does baptism bring about?

4. What does Luther mean when he says that free will is "pure fiction" and that our faith makes baptism meaningful and fruitful for us?

6

Baptism and Infants

Why Do We Baptize Whom We Baptize?

"Do children believe, and is it right to baptize them?" asked Luther in his *Large Catechism*. This would be of interest to any parent concerned about his or her child's faith and fate. It became one of the burning questions of the day after the Anabaptists—the re-baptizers—discontinued infant baptism and preached that a demonstration of faith was required before baptism. Given all the emphasis Luther himself assigned to faith in his theology as a whole, the question targets the heart of the matter: why do we baptize who we baptize and what role does faith play?

Luther's discussion of infant baptism might seem at first patronizing, for he wrote that the issue of baptizing children was better left for the learned, and that "simple" people should not worry about it too much. But then Luther changed his tone: "That the baptism of infants is pleasing to Christ is sufficiently proved from his own work. God has sanctified many who have been thus baptized and has given them the Holy Spirit." The experience of earlier Christians is the main proof. If God had not accepted infant baptism, then God would not have given God's blessings and the Holy Spirit to those so baptized in the past.[1] God, who does not like heresies, said Luther, clearly blessed infant baptism by allowing it to continue and by sanctifying it; this is evidenced in the success and continuity of the Christian church. This tradition alone is a reason enough to continue infant baptism.

Having made this basic point, Luther proceeded to clarify a couple of specific issues for his readers. First, he maintained that baptism is a gift that does not depend on our own faith or earnest belief. "For my faith does not make baptism; rather, it receives baptism," wrote Luther.

"Baptism does not become invalid if it is not properly received or used, as I have said, for it is not bound to our faith but to the Word."[2] According to Luther, our faith exists not for the sake of baptism but, rather, baptism exists for the sake of faith.

Second, Luther went to great length to illustrate God's graciousness and action versus our neediness and passivity in justification, most clearly manifest in baptism. Salvation is a gift; baptism is a gift. We can only receive it—and then all we can do is "have faith" in what already is. To "have faith" means to draw spiritually from the belief that makes baptism meaningful for us. The saving kind of faith—faith beyond our belief—is something that is given and is of divine origin. Stressing this, Luther underscored here the absolute gift nature of our divine restoration.

Even the saving kind of faith has to be given to us. This makes sense in light of how Luther taught that our salvation and justification—that is, our being forgiven and made right in a restored relationship with our maker—is "by faith alone" rather than merited with our efforts. It is always a gift of God's unconditional grace, given for us who need it but who do not necessarily even know to "want" or ask for right things. The gift of salvation begins from the gift of faith, and it is given equally to all, even to infants—especially to infants. Otherwise, who could be baptized and saved? Who would be so worthy?

The baptism of infants is a case in point about how baptism works for any of us. The helpless state of infants illustrates well our inability to produce a saving kind of faith. Like infants, in our faith we also exist in a state of dependence; we need constantly to "receive." Babies, just like any of us, can be baptized exactly because baptism does not rely on our human faith or effort. Our own faith does not make baptism; God does, through God's Word. Specifically, "baptism is simply water and God's Word in and with each other; that is, when the Word accompanies the water, baptism is valid, even though faith is lacking."[3]

The Word that functions in baptism is a particular word—it is Christ Jesus who welcomed children and sinners to his company. It is Christ who established baptism and gives it its meaning and an invitation to it. The very practice of infant baptism is a testimony of our holding on to God's promise of grace for the whole world and to our belief that grace has already entered the world in the work and person of Christ. Because of our certainty about Christ and what Christ has completed once and for all as our redeemer, we can believe with absolute certainty the validity of baptism for even an oblivious baby. There is no need to perform a better baptism later or to make sure the baptized has the right kind of faith about the ritual. Just as what Christ did in his death and resurrection need not be repeated, there is no need to repeat baptism. It is a "done deal."

This participation has no prerequisites—which is good because we could not do what Christ has done. Because of what we believe about Christ and the completeness of his saving work for us, we can and we should baptize infants, regardless of what we think about their ability to have faith or understanding. The little infants remind us that all that we need in baptism takes place and is given in baptism itself. What is promised, happens, and we simply cannot spoil this "good thing"; we have no power to ruin what God has made, any more than infants can ruin their own DNA or birth. This is good news for us!

After declaring that faith is actually a non-factor in the effectiveness of baptism, Luther went on to emphasize the need to teach the importance of faith, so that the merits of baptism might become real for us personally. While baptism does not depend on faith and while faith does not exist for the sake of baptism but the other way around, baptism does become complete with faith, wrote Luther. Is this a contradiction? No, it is a positive ambiguity between what is already and what can be and will unfold for us. There is no ambiguity about God's intent and promise. With this knowledge, "We bring the child with the intent and hope that it may believe, and we pray God to grant it faith. But we do not baptize on this basis, but solely on the command of God. Why? Because we know that God does not lie."[4]

Because of what we believe about God and about Jesus in particular, we can be sure of the power of baptism. Luther's arguments on this matter crystallized very much during the time he defended the practice against the beliefs of the Anabaptists. Their teaching that baptism could be redone to make sure of it being right and effective violated

Luther's basic beliefs about God's steadfastness and the gift nature of grace. He also worried about a sacrament of grace being made into a requirement or an achievement or a word of law. His primary concern was to emphasize that we simply cannot mess up, nor should we try to put any conditions on God's grace and God's salvation. "For God's ordinance and Word cannot be changed or altered by human beings."[5] Fortunately so!

When Is Baptism Certain and Right?

In his *Concerning Rebaptism* Luther fleshed out similar points, addressing the counter-arguments of the Anabaptists in earnest. First of all, he dealt with the question of how we know that we are baptized for certain. His answer was simple: from the witness of other people. As our birth is public, so is our baptism. It can be remembered and verified by others as fact. This public knowledge is for the benefit and comfort of our weak faith most of all. We need not second-guess what has already taken place for us. The collective memory works for our benefit here.

Second, Luther emphasized that baptism is the work of God, commanded by God. For us to be baptized is a privilege for which none of us is worthy. If there were among us anyone more worthy of baptism than others, it would be infants first and foremost as they cannot deceive! We cannot deceive God, we cannot fake our worthiness for baptism, we cannot present ourselves to God in favorable light any more than newborn babies can. They are our best examples of who is worthy of God's love. This simple insight Luther developed while observing his own children, and it is a powerful insight for us to remember any time we find ourselves worrying about our worthiness or about the validity of our baptism.

Third, Luther drew explanation from the Scriptures. In Matthew 19:14, Jesus commanded, "Let the little children come to me, and do not stop them; for it is to such as these that the kingdom of heaven belongs." And again in Matthew 28:19, Christ commanded, "Go . . . and make disciples of all nations, baptizing them." All people—children, men and women, Jews, Gentiles—everybody, with no discrimination whatsoever in terms of who might merit such a gift may be invited to the company of Jesus.

On the subject of faith and infants in particular, Luther made several conclusions. First, there simply is no proof that children do not have faith. In the lack of proof that children do not believe, we should assume the opposite. Second, baptism is ultimately not about faith but about salvation, the critical concern for which we should err on the side of generosity rather than frugality. Baptism is to be dished out, not parceled. "For even if I were not sure that they believed, yet for my children's sake I would have to let them be baptized," wrote Luther. "I would much rather allow them baptism than to keep them from it. For if, as we believe, baptism is right and useful and brings the children to salvation, and I then did away with it, then I would be responsible for all the children who were lost because they were unbaptized—a cruel and terrible thing."[6] In other words, baptism will hurt no one, whereas neglecting to offer it might hurt us. Our job is to make sure baptism is available for everyone.

While remaining somewhat vague here about the issue of infants' faith but going on record for being more than willing to entertain the possibility of it, Luther reasoned that just as God has established that Christians everywhere accept the Bible and the Lord's Prayer as our prayer, we should accept the faith of a child as genuine faith. Why? Luther answered by reminding us of who is behind baptism and its benefits—God. Thus, "It is likewise the work of God that during all the time children were being baptized, he [God] has given great and holy gifts to many of them, enlightened and strengthened them with the Holy Spirit and understanding of the Scripture, and accomplished great things in Christendom through them."[7] The issue of infant baptism becomes a case in point to highlight again what baptism, what grace, is about: God's act, God's work, God coming to us.

Issues of Emergency and Earnest Prayer

When the reformers wrote about baptism, they often were addressing specific life situations and thinking of real infants, most certainly so when approached by parents with questions such as, "What will happen to my child? What can we do?" More often than we would like to think, people faced having a child die "prematurely" (and when would death not be premature, in human perspective, we might add) and without baptism. Or in other cases, a child may have been baptized in an emergency and parents wondered about the validity of such baptism, or a child was delivered by an Anabaptist midwife and they were not sure if she had indeed baptized the failing infant, and if so, in time and appropriately. (It did not help that cases had been reported of midwives caught lying about baptisms that never took place, in the hope of a "proper" baptism taking place later!) Of continuous concern was the validity of baptism performed by lay persons without the qualifications of ordination or theological degree, and perhaps with unverifiable or questionable rituals. People wondered whether there be any harm, or benefit, in repeating or redoing the baptism if the child survived after all.

These issues ring true in our world as well. Just ask any hospital chaplain or intern or nurse to share stories of the many emergency baptisms performed and the many requests from grief-struck parents for a baptism of their stillborn child. In accordance with Lutheran teaching, what do we think of emergency baptism? Do we really need it? Or, can a person be baptized more than once? Are there invalid baptisms? What if we are not sure if we were ever baptized and cannot prove it? What might God do with us in such cases?

Luther and his contemporaries firmly believed that baptism was necessary for salvation, for in baptism one becomes a child of God, sealed with God's kiss, member of God's family, forgiven and purified, and thus an inheritor of eternal life. No light matters at stake. It was also believed that baptism would cleanse us from sin like nothing else, and that every one of us needed that because of the original sin. The Catholic Church's teaching about limbo did little to ease the minds of parents. The idea of un-baptized infants not being allowed into heaven but transferred instead to a special place—limbo—accompanied by the practice of burying unbaptized children outside the churchyard, was not at all comforting. Rather, it caused much anxiety in people's minds.

Luther and the reformers proposed some big changes in this regard, starting with eliminating the place called limbo from their vocabulary and their theological imagination. Only two options were imagined for after death: heaven or hell, the company of God and all God's angels and saints or the dark opposite. Belief in both remained solid during the Reformation, and lasts today, even if we are less eager to try to imagine hell and even if we understand heaven as a reality not tied to any spatial location. Regardless of how we view the existence of heaven as the company of God, and regardless of how we view the possibility of hell as the place without God and goodness, when it comes to baptism, this can become the bottom line issue: is this rite in any way decisive in "where we go from here," that is, does it determine our eternal fate and existence?

Luther wrote tender words offering a most inclusive vision of God's grace in response to the earnest and heartbreaking concerns of grieving parents whose children had died without being baptized. A situation like that would cause tremendous anxiety in the minds of people feeling themselves so far from God's mercy when staring death in the eye. Luther has left us a treatise where he addressed grieving women[8] who had buried their children with their tears and prayers, while torn by uncertainty (only enhanced by the traditional teaching of limbo and hell). In this treatise it becomes evident how much Luther approached the issue of baptism and grace and children "out of the box," especially so when writing as a pastor rather than a theologian in battle mode. In these conversations Luther's vision of God's grace is at its most compassionate and creative, while not departing from his overall teaching of baptism and grace and the power of sacraments. Always emphasizing God's mercy and desire to love us, when finding words to comfort mothers who feared for the eternal fate of their children, Luther imagined a full spectrum of God's ways to bring us into God's grace. Luther saw this inclusion to grace happening both through our holy rituals and preaching the Word, but also in other ways, in ways beyond what we can imagine or even hope.

For instance, according to Luther, tears of grieving mothers could serve the same purpose as baptism. He also believed in the power of the parents' "spiritual yearning" (as in the case of the widow of Nain whose son was awakened because of his mother's longing and not the son's faith in Luke 7:11-17). Another way to think about this is to consider faith exactly in light of what is meaningful for us personally: our belief in being baptized is enough evidence to believe that we indeed have been for all purposes baptized and can personally benefit from all the gifts baptism offers—even if it ends up being the case that we actually were never baptized with the customary ritual. Luther even went so far as to say that, in the end, even if only one person was baptized, that would cover all of us for God's benign purposes and in God's mysterious design.

The core truth for Luther the pastor and Luther the theologian was this: God alone saves us and brings us to God; without God our rituals are empty and bring about nothing. By the same token, God can also work without our rituals and means, God being all-powerful and slipping through our human-made constructions. Another principal truth for Luther was in the words "for me"—as long as we are drawn closer to God and are finding the personal assurance of grace, by whatever means that may be, that is a goal and a gain in itself.

In his advice for women who had lost their children to death before baptism, Luther was very much attuned to the issue of what this tragedy meant for parents, and he was careful to find the word of gospel for them. In their sorrowful situation where they saw little hope but were hanging on to their faith that God might hear their prayers, undeserved as they might be, Luther's most comforting message to these women was that God has many ways to "save" us and come to us. Furthermore, we should know that as much as God wants us to call upon God, should we fail to do that, God is already speaking on behalf of us. (That is, God is speaking to God about us!) God goes so far for us, or God comes so close to us and our situations. Luther reminded the women, and us, that our God is always prepared and steps ahead of us in terms of what we might think we need. "The immeasurable does more than we either ask or conceive," Luther quoted from Scripture.[9]

In this regard, we should be at ease when imagining how God approaches our little ones. First of all, we should be comforted by the knowledge that our prayers are pleasing to God. This is so regardless of who we are or how well we pray and what our concerns might be. Second, we should be comforted by the knowledge that God heard us before we even prayed, because God has already prayed for us before we even take a breath to do so. In terms of what this means for the children we worry about, this much is clear: "Therefore, we should present such cases [unbaptized infants] to God and console ourselves that [God] assuredly hears our unspoken longings and has done everything better than we have been able to put into words. In sum, take special care to be a true Christian and thus to pray in proper faith to God and learn to yearn from your heart, whether in this or any other distress. Then do not be sorry and do not worry, either for your child or for yourself. Know that your prayer is pleasing and that God will do everything much better than you can grasp or desire. 'Call upon me,' [God] says in Psalm 50, 'and I will help you; you should praise and thank me.'"[10]

In light of Luther's words, then, since God is this compassionate and creative in bringing us into grace, should we not also then strive to relate with similar grace and compassion to our fellow human beings? Should we not keep Luther's creative, compassionate words of grace in mind when teaching and preaching and offering the means of grace? We could be bold like Luther and simply assume that since we don't know God's secret judgments and don't control God's ways, we cannot bind God's own promise to any ritual, no matter how important or dear we hold the ritual for us. In our limited judgments, we can only keep in mind how unbelievably graceful God is. We have plenty of evidence for that from Scripture.

For Reflection and Discussion

1. What would be the ideal age to bring a child to baptism? What role does the child's faith play in baptism being "real"?

2. If you are a grandparent and your grandchild remains unbaptized, should you worry about his or her eternal fate and relationship with God?

3. What is an emergency baptism? Who qualifies to perform one? For instance, should the emergency room nurse baptize a failing infant?

4. Could baptism ever be invalid? Would there ever be grounds to re-baptize?

7

Baptism as the Basis for Spiritual Living

Sinner's Holiness

Luther's most important lens for spiritual living is his famous insight that in this life we are simultaneously saints and sinners. Pairing the words *sinner* and *saint* describes the reality of every baptized person and what constitutes spiritual living as one who, on the one hand, is prone to sin and frequently slips away from God's intentions, and who, on the other hand, is already totally forgiven and holy. Luther's vision is radically different from the way his contemporaries thought about holiness and sin. In the medieval religious imagination, some people were simply regarded better than others, as if they lived their lives with more grace and could reach closer to God. Saints were people with special graces and next to God. Ordinary people could hardly expect to reach such a status and intimacy with the Divine. The standards were simply too hard, and their sins, too many. Luther, himself frustrated with the ideals and knowing himself as a sinner first and foremost, began to preach equal-opportunity grace and democratic holiness: we are all equally sinners and we are all equally holy. Suddenly holiness and wholeness came within the reach of each baptized person.

Given Luther's lens that we are simultaneously saints and sinners, what kind of holiness and wholeness can we hope for in this life? In Luther's view, holiness is always broken holiness, finite holiness, and it never leads to our perfection or becoming better than others. Holiness of a sinner-saint is dependent completely on the mercy of God, who alone can make sinners whole and holy and who does so without any conditions, regardless of what we deserve. Thus, a Lutheran vision of spiritual living is life lived in a tension of "already" and "not yet"—already being made fully holy and yet engaged in an ongoing struggle with sin that prevents us from resting on our holy laurels and makes us needful of constant renewal and assurance of forgiveness. Traditionally, Lutherans tend to identify more comfortably with the designation of sinner than that of saint, and we are uneasy with too much talk about spiritual growth—the life-long process of maturing in Christian living that is called sanctification. But, Lutherans are eager to speak of the gifts that God showers upon us in baptism, and for this reason, baptism is the perfect place to begin to reclaim the words *saints* and *holiness* for our Lutheran vocabulary and our spiritual imagination. Here, too, we can begin to lift up the work of the Holy Spirit and our experiences of life in the Spirit, which our Evangelical Christian sisters and brothers speak of so freely. Baptism is the place to start as we seek ways to live intentionally Spirit-filled and Spirit-directed lives with a sense of wholeness that comes from connecting with both the tangible and less tangible aspects of our lives.

Holiness of Gratitude and Servanthood

With Luther we believe that baptism makes us right with God, and in baptism, God who is Spirit comes into our lives and makes our lives like that of Christ's. In baptism we are united on a personal level with God and are made holy; we are not just regarded and "seen" as holy but transformed into Christ's image. If this were not so, God, who is holy, could not dwell in us.

With Luther, we believe, too, that baptism does not remove all that makes us wander away from the home we have in God and the purpose God imparts to our lives. Baptism does not make us immune to falls or errors or hurt or death, nor does it make us better than others. Instead, baptism reminds us that in this life, where sin clings so closely, we live in God's presence even as we await a new life where there is no hurt or sorrow, where there is no sin and we sinner-saints have become saints of God in all meanings of the word. We believe that this holiness and this hope of eternity is given to us in baptism. And we believe that we cannot in any way make it happen anymore than we can keep it from happening. We simply cannot spoil God's good work.

Our holiness is an "alien" holiness, given to us because of Jesus alone. In his explanation of the Apostles' Creed Luther reminded that while baptism brings us to righteousness and holiness and keeps us there, it is always God who does all this, and our holiness is always from God. According to Luther: "I believe that by my own understanding or strength I cannot believe in Jesus Christ my Lord or come to him, but instead the Holy Spirit has called me through the gospel, enlightened me with his gifts, made me holy and kept me in the true faith, just as [the Spirit] calls, gathers, enlightens, and makes holy the whole Christian church."[1] With his holiness comes the commission to live according to his example, for to be holy like Jesus means being oriented to serving as he served.

As recipients of unbelievable generosity and compassion from our maker, we are oriented to give in return. Any goodness that we extend to others isn't our own doing, but is God's own Spirit working through us. The Spirit stirs up in us a compassion and generosity of spirit that we cannot create on our own and that, in turn, we offer to others from the position of humble gratitude for all we have been given. Such holiness, as Luther envisioned it, is dynamic and transforming. It is about action, not status. It is active because of the Spirit who is active in us.

Sanctified by the Spirit

Luther did not often lift up the role of the Holy Spirit explicitly, but he did so when imagining how the work of the Holy Spirit in baptism makes us holy. For instance, he wrote, "But God's Spirit alone is called a Holy Spirit, that is, the one who has made us holy and still makes us holy . . . the Holy Spirit must be called a Sanctifier, or one who makes us holy."[2] The implications of this are enormously important. For one, we believe that because of the Spirit, we can enjoy the full, all-permeating presence of God in our whole lives. There is no place where God cannot be and where God cannot meet us. Second, we believe that the Holy Spirit enables us to live more fully. Through the many ways the Spirit works for us we are made increasingly conscious of the spiritual in our lives, that is, all that is of and from God, a reality for which we get a taste in this life and to which we will belong fully in the next.

When explaining the holiness and sanctity brought about by the Holy Spirit, Luther presented a very practical question that is helpful for trying to understand the role of baptism in our context: "How does such sanctifying take place?" In other words, through what means and in what contexts does the Holy Spirit work? Luther answered, "[The] Holy Spirit effects our being made holy through the following: the community of saints or Christian church, the forgiveness of sins, the resurrection of the body, and the life everlasting."[3]

The means by which and the contexts within which the Holy Spirit works in the work of the church are, in one way or another, all linked to the sacrament of baptism. How is this so? Baptism is a sacrament of the church and it is into the church that we are baptized. But, in addition to the gift of belonging to the church—the communion of saints—that the sacrament brings, baptism is instrumental in bringing the gift of forgiveness and the promises of resurrection and eternal life to us. These are the very things, as we confess in the Creeds, that we believe God provides. At the same time, these gifts are a part and result of the proclamation of the gospel. Baptism is about gospel just as much as the gospel gives baptism its meaning. Through Word and water—a spiritual element and a material element—God the Spirit comes to us in ways that we can't even begin to imagine. Baptism is a special intersection for the spiritual and the physical in our lives, and it involves our whole being, spirit and body alike. The Word, doing the work of the Spirit, is the connector or the hinge.

When explaining how the gospel Word works to bring the presence of God into our lives, Luther revealed that holiness, just as forgiveness promised in the gospel, is brought about by concrete means of grace that have been given for our benefit and use.[4] While baptism is one of the central means of grace, it is by no means the only one, nor does it work by itself. What makes baptism special is the Word of God that acts as a driving force to bring the grace from God to where it is needed. Luther wrote in *Smalcald Articles*, "Moreover, the gospel does not give consolation and forgiveness in only one way—but rather through the Word, sacraments, and the like."[5] He identified for his readers some of the specific ways through which we can encounter the gospel and be touched by the grace it conveys: "first, through the spoken word, in which the forgiveness of sins is preached to the whole world (which is the proper function of the gospel); second, through baptism; third, through the holy Sacrament of the Altar; fourth, through the power of the keys and also through the mutual conversation and consolation of brothers and sisters."[6]

It was important for Luther to point out that baptism, as a specific means of grace and as a medium for holiness and the presence of the Holy Spirit, becomes effective and meaningful when used in the context it was given for: the church, the community of believers. The church has been a particular operating place for the Holy Spirit since the event of the first Pentecost, which is understood traditionally as the day the Christian church was born. It is within the church that Christians baptize new members into life in the Spirit and commit to proclaiming the good news, the Word. (This was, after all, the very reason why the church was instituted.)

Spirituality and Trinity

For Luther, spirituality is life with God in a personal, intimate relationship where God is the giver and we are the receivers. Lutheran spirituality is Trinitarian; it is based on God our creator who has given us life, Christ our redeemer who restores us to a forgiven relationship where we are loved because of God's own work, and the Spirit our sustainer who fills us with God and keeps us close to God and who directs us according to God's desires for us in this life, even as we falter. In the Lutheran view of spirituality we cannot make ourselves better or more able to reach God; rather, we are constantly re-awakened to a realization that God has come to us and is waiting for us to experience more fully the blessings that come from an intimate union with our creator who has a "job" for us all.

How Luther explained our relationship with God has everything to do with the work and person of Jesus Christ, who has made it possible for us to be loved by God in the first place, sinners as we are.

Namely, according to Luther, when God sees us, God sees only Christ. Where this all comes to be ours and lived out by us is in the work of the Holy Spirit. Baptism more than anything invites us to appreciate specifically the role of the Holy Spirit in our lives. The lasting effects of baptism are tied to the work of the Spirit who lives with us and sustains us in the daily struggles as Christians trying to follow Christ's model and live out his teachings. We cannot understand how the benefits of Christ's work and the qualities of Christ's person come to us in baptism without looking at the work of the Spirit, and we cannot see the life of the baptized as anything else but as life with the Spirit.

Equality in Spiritual Living

Luther's vision of spiritual living was revolutionary in his sixteenth-century context. He changed the notion of holiness and what is meant by spirituality.[7] For one, no longer was holiness and closeness to God seen as belonging to the spiritual elite, that is, to the monks and nuns, the contemplative and ascetic individuals who opted to exclude themselves from the "world" and every day life in order to deliberately aim for special closeness with God. In Luther's world these individuals were typically viewed as "better" and holier in comparison to "ordinary" Christians. One of the assumptions behind medieval Christian theology and religious practice and the understanding of holiness was that persons could and should try to reach higher, to reach closeness with God by special methods, with the help of grace of course. In this model, there would remain hierarchies between individuals reaching this goal in different degrees. Some people would be closer to God and express godly ideals better than others. The changes for an "ordinary" person to become considered "saintly" were minuscule.

Luther's idea of spiritual equality, that all believers are equally close to God—or, on their own, equally distant from God—was a startling change in this regard. Luther's understanding of the gospel in light of the sinful human condition in bondage to sin made him conclude that believers were equal and in equal need of God's saving grace. According to Luther's teaching, nobody can reach God on his or her own; it is impossible because of sin that affects everyone in this life. There are no pure saints in that regard. There are only "sinning saints." To Luther, closeness to God and even union with God is equally possible for everyone. This is so only and explicitly because of God's own act and will. God's will is not predisposed to grant grace to some individuals more than to others. God's grace is free and for all to whom the gospel is preached and to whom the sacraments are administered. We could add here that certainly the gospel, the Word, the medium of the invisible Spirit, also has other ways to reach us, without being limited to any particular ritual or format.

Baptism is given to humankind, Luther believed, in order to bring us closer to God and to assist us in the faith that we need to live a spiritually meaningful life. In baptism we connect with God the Spirit, and the spiritual dimension of life opens up for us in an entirely new way. In baptism we connect in ways that matter beyond the visible. This connection that emerges from the combination of water and Word, realized in faith that God will use this channel for God's own purposes of dishing out grace to us personally, is life-giving and life-changing. Being baptized is as if being plugged into an electrical outlet; it is up to us to leave the switch on or off.

Luther gives us many reasons to remember our baptismal date, to return to the child's question about why the date is so important. The date reminds us concretely that we have received holiness and become filled with the Holy Spirit, and thus, full of God. It reminds us of the life we are invited to, of the special mission of compassion we are initiated into as baptized Christians. It reminds us of the fact that we are living a life spiritual, plugged into the Spirit and have there a dimension to our existence that is big enough to explore the rest of our lives. It reminds us that with such holy life comes a holy purpose and responsibility—to convey now to the world in which we live that godly grace and goodness, love and "alien holiness" we have undeservedly received, to enable and allow transformations of various sort to take place where they are needed.

For Reflection and Discussion

1. What does baptism-based spirituality look and feel like?

2. How can we deepen our awareness of the meaning of baptism and what are some of the ways in which we can "live it out" in a larger sense in our private lives, in our faith community, and in the world?

3. How can we appreciate or experience our "union" with God?

4. What does baptism teach us about the Holy Spirit and compassion?

8

Considerations for Today

Throughout Christian history baptism has been the most commonly practiced Christian ritual, even while being a continuing source of contention among Christians who have not always agreed in the past and do not agree now on its meaning or practice. This has been the case particularly since the Protestant Reformations in the sixteenth century, prior to which Christian baptism was legislated and was largely part and parcel of obedience to the uniform teachings of the "one" church and the binding law of the empire. In spite of different emphases about the meaning of baptism, however, a couple of points of continuity have characterized the sacrament from the time when Christianity was a fledgling community of believers until today when Christianity has global presence and claims more adherents than any other religion:

- Baptism involves an intentional use of water and calls for the presence of Jesus, in whose memory we baptize.
- Baptism is connected to Scripture, from which the incentive for the practice comes and in which is found the promise of new life that baptism brings.

Spiritual Choices

Baptism is as important today as it was in the past, but perhaps now it is more a matter of personal spirituality than denominational loyalty. This shift reflects the increased emphasis on spirituality that is prevalent in both the religious and secular cultures of our time. Given the diversity of spiritual practices today, we who live in the twenty-first century have choices that earlier generations did not have about where to find our religious homes and what forms of spirituality to embrace. Even within the Christian faith, choices abound on everything from ethical and theological convictions to styles of worship. Pertinent to baptism specifically, such choices include where, when, why, and how to baptize. The choices also include different approaches to what it means to "live spiritually" once we are baptized and what meaningful spiritual living looks like. Today baptism is a deeply spiritual matter, where ultimate concerns rather than human-made conventions are at stake.

For Christians, baptism is the place to begin our search for spiritual wholeness and godly meaning and purposeful direction for our lives. It is a lens through which we see ourselves having a personal place in God's creation and a lens through which we discern how God acts in our lives and in the world through us. In baptism God provides a tangible and precious means to help us stay focused on what God offers us. In baptism God provides the stimulus to better understand what life in a personal "baptized" relationship with God entails—what daily life with the Spirit means for us.

Lutherans Continue to Baptize

Lutherans teach about the meaning and importance of baptism in the spirit of Martin Luther, who presented it as a sacrament—a means of grace—and advised believers to hold on to it with an unwavering faith, trusting firmly in its plentiful blessings. Luther saw in baptism unconditional forgiveness, restored relationship and union with God, and holiness with the entrance of the Holy Spirit. Luther lifted up "a jewel in a jewel" by pointing out that in the humble water of baptism the God who made us, saves us, and enables us to grow in faith comes to be with us. The full God—Creator, Redeemer, and Sanctifier—claims the baptized, and we are transformed into oneness with Christ. Empowered by God's Spirit, we live a new life.

Lutherans have been baptizing for more than 500 years, guided by a vision of God who loves us freely and reconciles us to God out of pure grace. Today one of the challenges in our spiritually diverse world is how to continue confidently to uphold and share the promises we believe baptism carries, but doing so with compassion and respect for the authenticity of other spiritual understandings and experiences of God and God's grace. As Scripture reminds us, we do not have a monopoly on God's blessings and presence: "God so loved the *world*" (John 3:16, emphasis added). Jesus came into the world to reveal through his teaching, his example, and his death and resurrection God's all-encompassing and all-healing love. And it is into the world—*to all nations*—that Jesus sends us to proclaim the gospel, to teach, and to baptize (see Matt. 28:19). It would seem warranted to be very cautious that we do not turn what in this life is a rite of *inclusion* into the Christian faith into a rite of *exclusion* in terms of life in the world to come. In the spirit of Jesus, are we not challenged to focus our attention on better understanding the ways of God's grace in the world, in our shared lives, and in the means at our disposal to share God's grace? Always keeping in mind that stewardship—not gatekeeping—is expected from us, are we not urged to excel in caring for the precious jewel given to us in baptism and in sharing its promises with a spiritually hungry world?

In the baptismal liturgy used in many Lutheran churches, the newly baptized is presented with a lighted candle and admonished to "[l]et your light so shine before others that they may see your good works and glorify your Father in heaven."[1] As much as baptism is a gift to us personally, it is also a gift to the world. As recipients not only of God's gifts but of God's Spirit in baptism, and as instruments of God's love and grace for all people, we can participate in making room in the world today for the kingdom Jesus promised. The rest is God's doing.

Stewardship of the Jewel

It is no small thing to care for such a treasure! Baptism belongs to the life and use of the church, which, by Lutheran definition, is the people of God gathered around Word and sacrament. But the church does not exist unto itself; the church exists to bring the gospel to the world. We will find many opportunities to connect on the concerns and values we share with people whose spiritual journeys follow paths different from our own. Impelled by virtue of being baptized, we can bear witness to the promise we have embraced from God who loved the world so much that God sent Jesus to be one of us, the same Jesus in whose name we are baptized and after whose command we are sent out with the "good news."

As Christians, we proclaim that the gift of baptism grants such blessings and privileges as protection, sustenance, hope, and a godly perspective for our lives in days of joy and sorrow. These blessings and privileges are not limited; they are for everyone. Even if Christian baptism and the gospel are deliberately Jesus-centered, in the sacrament we receive benefits that are universally desirable and pertinent. Who would not want security against all that threatens to harm them? Who would not be at least curious about something that could bring fulfillment in life? Safety from harm and care and guidance in difficult situations are certainly universal aspirations, as is the quest for a meaningful existence and "divine purpose" in the ups and downs of life.

We proclaim that baptism offers all this, but does what we proclaim show in the way we live? How does baptism change the world where we offer it? Is baptism or being baptized a stimulus for positive transformations and promoting goodness in the world? It should be. Otherwise it would seem we have failed to be good stewards of the treasures given to us. As much as we are well served by seeking a deeper understanding of the meaning of baptism "for me" and "for us" specifically, we are better stewards of the gift if we also earnestly imagine what our baptism means in the bigger picture, in light of the well-being of God's creation and all humankind. This expectation is imbedded in our baptismal ritual: The Service for Holy Baptism in *Evangelical Lutheran Worship* includes among the responsibilities of the baptized, to "trust God, proclaim Christ through word and deed, care for others and the world God made, and work for justice and peace."[2] Given how much is at stake, surely we would like to invest the treasure wisely and use the gift for the purposes the "donor" intended. Surely we would want to participate in the fulfillment of God's kingdom on earth, which Jesus promised when he sent his disciples to baptize.

While we can be proud of the jewel we have in our possession, at the same time, we need to keep in mind that all the gifts given to us by God are intended for the good of all creation. And as baptized children of God, we are called to be servants in this world. As Luther taught, our holiness is based on the divine model of servanthood; our holiness entails caring for others with compassion, with love that resonates with the love of God for the world. But we have a fundamental difficulty with this: we would rather not care for the others. That is our inherited sin. That is also why we need baptism—so that we can even *want* to care and be part of what God wants for us and from us.

Baptism is a good starting point for us to reflect on what we are about as Christians, as baptized Christians, with the incredible good news to share with the world. Our baptism reminds us of the divine care shown to us, and in turn, the care we are to show others, just as Jesus did. Even with our imperfections, we can make a difference, together. We can, because we are empowered to do so by God who cares for us and claims us in baptism. We can because of the Spirit of God who in baptism has come to stay in us.

A child's innocent question, "What's so important about my baptismal date?" is a poignant one. Recalling that particular date when the Christian story became real and meaningful for us—"for me"—means remembering everything. We remember what we believe about God and God's hopes for us. We remember the world's ills and the remedies and responses we have for them. We remember our responsibilities as those who have been entrusted with a treasure. It's a little like taking the family diamond out of the jewelry box, dusting it for another look, and once again standing in awe of its beauty. It is all about remembering a treasure too precious to be hidden or forgotten!

For Reflection and Discussion

1. Are there "wrong" or ineffective baptisms? Are there people who should not be baptized?

2. How can we interpret Jesus' command to "go and baptize" in today's world where not everybody aspires to be a follower of Jesus or reads the same Holy Scripture?

3. What do we mean when we say "But we are baptized!"?

4. How are you being a good steward of the treasure you have been given? How are you living out your baptism?

Notes

Introduction

1. Martin Luther, *Large Catechism*, in Robert Kolb and Timothy Wengert, eds., *The Book of Concord (New Translation): The Confessions of the Evangelical Lutheran Church* (Minneapolis: Fortress Press, 2000), 461.

2. Ibid.

Chapter 1

1. For instance, see Matthew 28 and Matthew 3. See the baptismal rituals recorded in the Acts 8:36-37; Acts 8:12-13; Acts 2:41; Acts 9:18; Acts 10:47-48; Acts 16:15; Acts 16:33; Acts 18:8; 1 Corinthians 1:14-16; John 3:22-26.

2. Peter John Cramer, *Baptism in the Early Middle Ages, c. 200-c.1150* (Cambridge: Cambridge University Press, 1993), 10-14.

3. See Bryan D. Spinks, *Early and Medieval Rituals and Theologies of Baptism: From the New Testament to the Council of Trent* (Aldershot, UK/Burlington, Vt.: Ashgate, 2006), vol. 1, 64-67.

4. From the first seven ecumenical councils of the church come our basic definition of God as the Trinity, and our doctrines about Christ's person as simultaneously human and divine and about Christ as the savior of the humankind bereaved by original sin, and about the role of the Holy Spirit and the Church in mediating grace. Sometimes doctrinal decisions have followed already-in-place practices, while at the same time the church's doctrinal preferences have shaped the practices and teaching of the holy rituals, such as baptism.

5. On the development of the rite in the medieval western church, see Spinks, *Early and Medieval Rituals and Theologies of Baptism*, 134-156; also Cramer, *Baptism in the Early Middle Ages*, 125-130.

6. Since the Eastern Emperor Justinian (died 565 c.e.), all Christians belonging to the church catholic were to be baptized, according to the Justinian codex of law. From the sixth century on, the law in the empire decreed mandatory baptism, with penalties that followed a failure to comply.

Chapter 2

1. Martin Luther, *The Heidelberg Disputation*, 1518, Article 19-21 in particular, in Timothy Lull, ed., *Martin Luther's Basic Theological Writings* (Minneapolis:

Fortress Press, 2005), 58. For those readers interested in reading what Luther had to say about baptism in his own words, Timothy Lull's edition of Luther's writings is recommended as a whole, as it contains a solid selection of Luther's theologically most pertinent writings, also about baptism, and is the most user-friendly collection available.

2. Martin Luther, *Booklet on Baptism* 1523, in Robert Kolb and Timothy Wengert, eds., *The Book of Concord* (Minneapolis: Fortress Press, 2000), 372.

3. Ibid, 372-373.

4. Jaroslav Pelikan and Helmut T. Lehman, eds., *Luther's Works: American Edition* (Philadelphia: Fortress Press, 1957-), 53:102; Epilogue to 1523 rite, quoted in Spinks, *Reformation and Modern Rituals and Theologies of Baptism: From Luther to Contemporary Practices* (Aldershot, UK/Burlington, Vt.: Ashgate, 2006), 2:11.

5. Luther, *Booklet on Baptism* 1523, in Kolb and Wengert, *The Book of Concord*, 372.

6. *Luther's Works* 53:103, quoted in Spinks, *Reformation and Modern Rituals and Theologies of Baptism*, 2:10.

Chapter 3

1. Martin Luther, *Large Catechism*, in Robert Kolb and Timothy Wengert, eds., *The Book of Concord (New Translation): The Confessions of the Evangelical Lutheran Church* (Minneapolis: Fortress Press, 2000), 458.

2. Ibid., 457.

3. Ibid.

4. Ibid., 461.

5. Ibid.

6. Ibid.

7. Ibid, 457, 461.

8. Ibid., 438.

9. Ibid., 459.

10. Ibid.

11. Ibid., 461.

Chapter 4

1. Martin Luther, *The Heidelberg Disputation*, 1518, Article 28, in Timothy Lull, ed., *Martin Luther's Basic Theological Writings* (Minneapolis: Fortress Press, 2005), 60.

2. Martin Luther, *Two Kinds of Righteousness*, 1519, in Lull, *Martin Luther's Basis Theological Writings*, 135.

3. For a pioneering work highlighting this important dimension in Luther's theology, see Tuomo Mannermaa, *Christ Present in Faith: Luther's View of Justification*, Translated and edited by Kirsi Stjerna. (Minneapolis: Fortress Press, 2005).

4. Martin Luther, *Two Kinds of Righteousness*, 1519, in Lull, *Martin Luther's Basis Theological Writings*, 135.

5. Ibid., 235-236.

6. *Evangelical Lutheran Worship* (Minneapolis: Augsburg Fortress Publishers, 2006), 231.

7. For a broad introduction to the mystics in Christian tradition, see Bernard McGinn, *The Essential Writings of Christian Mysticism*, (New York: The Modern Library, 2006), and the many volumes in the Paulist Press Series *The Classics of Western Spirituality*.

8. Martin Luther, *Two Kinds of Righteousness*, 1519, in Lull, *Martin Luther's Basis Theological Writings*, 135.

9. Martin Luther, *Large Catechism*, in Robert Kolb and Timothy Wengert, eds., *The Book of Concord (New Translation): The Confessions of the Evangelical Lutheran Church* (Minneapolis: Fortress Press, 2000), 466, in BOC.

10. Luther, *Large Catechism* (LC), 1529, 465.

11. Ibid., 466.

12. Ibid.

13. Martin Luther, *Large Catechism*, in Kolb and Wengert, eds., *The Book of Concord*, 466.

14. Ibid., 406.

15. Martin Luther, *Two Kinds of Righteousness*, 1519, in Lull, *Martin Luther's Basis Theological Writings*, 137.

16. Martin Luther, *Large Catechism*, in Kolb and Wengert, eds., *The Book of Concord*, 408.

17. Booklet on Baptism (BB), 1523, 375, in BOC.

18. Martin Luther, *Large Catechism*, in Kolb and Wengert, eds., *The Book of Concord*, 465.

19. Ibid., 461.

20. Ibid., 460.

21. Martin Luther, *Preface to Romans*, in Lull, *Martin Luther's Basis Theological Writings*, 101.

22. Martin Luther, *Large Catechism*, in Kolb and Wengert, eds., *The Book of Concord*, 406.

Chapter 5

1. *The Augsburg Confession*, contained in *The Book of Concord*, has twenty-eight articles that outline the Lutheran position on theological and practical issues, originally presented to the Emperor and the German princes at Augsburg in 1530, and from there on signed as the central confessional document for all Lutherans worldwide.

2. The German text was read at the original meeting at the Diet of Ausburg, the Latin version was prepared more for scholarly discussion. Our current English edition of *The Book of Concord* includes both translations.

3. *The Augsburg Confession*, in Robert Kolb and Timothy Wengert, eds., *The Book of Concord (New Translation): The Confessions of the Evangelical Lutheran Church* (Minneapolis: Fortress Press, 2000), 42.

4. Ibid., 32.

5. Martin Luther, *Smalcald Articles*, in Robert Kolb and Timothy Wengert, eds., *The Book of Concord* (Fortress Press, 2000), 348.

6. Martin Luther, *Bondage of the Will* in Timothy Lull, ed., *Martin Luther's Basic Theological Writings* (Minneapolis: Fortress Press, 2005), 168.

7. Ibid., 169.

8. Martin Luther, *Booklet on Baptism* 1523, in Robert Kolb and Timothy Wengert, eds., *The Book of Concord* (Fortress Press, 2000), 373.

9. Martin Luther, *Preface to Romans,* in Lull, *Martin Luther's Basic Theological Writings*, 101.

10. Martin Luther, *Large Catechism*, in Robert Kolb and Timothy Wengert, eds., *The Book of Concord* (Fortress Press, 2000), 459.

11. Ibid., 439.

12. Ibid., 432.

13. Martin Luther, *Smalcald Articles*, in Robert Kolb and Timothy Wengert, eds., *The Book of Concord* (Fortress Press, 2000), Art 5, Part III, 319-320.

14. Ibid., 320.

15. Martin Luther, *Large Catechism*, in Robert Kolb and Timothy Wengert, eds., *The Book of Concord* (Fortress Press, 2000), 460.

16. Martin Luther, *Booklet on Baptism* 1523, in Robert Kolb and Timothy Wengert, eds., *The Book of Concord* (Fortress Press, 2000), 373.

17. Martin Luther, *Large Catechism*, in Robert Kolb and Timothy Wengert, eds., *The Book of Concord* (Fortress Press, 2000), 462.

18. Martin Luther, *Booklet on Baptism* 1523, in Robert Kolb and Timothy Wengert, eds., *The Book of Concord* (Fortress Press, 2000), 373.

19. Ibid., 375. The prayer after the immersion stated that after hearing the word, "the Almighty God and Father of our Lord Jesus Christ, who has given birth to you for a second time through water and the Holy Spirit and has forgiven you all your sins, strengthen you with his grace to eternal life. Amen."

20. Ibid., 373.

Chapter 6

1. Martin Luther, *Large Catechism*, in Robert Kolb and Timothy Wengert, eds., *The Book of Concord* (Fortress Press, 2000), 462-463.

2. Ibid., 463.

3. Ibid.

4. Ibid., 464.

5. Ibid.

6. Martin Luther, *Concerning Rebaptism*, in Timothy Lull, ed., *Martin Luther's Basic Theological Writings* (Minneapolis: Fortress Press, 2005), 254.

7. Ibid., 255.

8. *Consolation to Those Women Who Have Had Difficulties in Bearing Children*, translated into English by Susann C. Karant-Nunn and Merrie E. Wiesner-Hanks, *Luther on Women, A Sourcebook* (Cambridge: Cambridge University Press, 2003), 180.

9. Ibid.

10. Ibid.

Chapter 7

1. Martin Luther, *Small Catechism*, in Robert Kolb and Timothy Wengert, eds., *The Book of Concord* (Fortress Press, 2000), 355.

2. Martin Luther, *Large Catechism*, in Kolb and Wengert, eds., *The Book of Concord*, 435.

3. Ibid.

4. Martin Luther, *Smallcald Articles*, Part III Art 4., in Kolb and Wengert, eds., *The Book of Concord*, 319.

5. Ibid., 313.

6. Ibid., 319. In "the Power of Keys" Luther referred to the traditionally recognized authority of those in the ministry to declare forgiveness of sins, following the authority Jesus gave to Peter with the "keys to the kingdom of heaven."

7. On reforms regarding spirituality, see Scott Hendrix, "Martin Luther's Reformation of Spirituality," in *Lutheran Quarterly* 13 (1999): 249-70, and in Timothy J. Wengert, ed., *Harvesting Martin Luther's Reflections on Theology, Ethics, and the Church* (Grand Rapids: Eerdmans, 2004), 240-260. The LTSG faculty book edited by Kirsi Stjerna and Brooks Schramm, *Spirituality, Toward a 21st Century Understanding* (Minneapolis: Lutheran University Press, 2004), offers different perspectives to reclaim the word *spirituality* into Lutheran thinking.

Chapter 8

1. *Evangelical Lutheran Worship* (Minneapolis: Augsburg Fortress Publishers, 2006), 231.

2. Ibid., 228.

Additional Resources

Selected Works from Luther

Lull, Timothy, ed. *Martin Luther's Basic Theological Writings*. Minneapolis: Fortress Press, 2005.

See especially *The Heidelberg Disputation* (1518), 47-61; *Two Kinds of Righteousness* (1519), 134-140; *On Christian Freedom* (1520), 386-411; *On Babylonian Captivity of the Church* (1520), 210-238; *Bondage of the Will* (1525), 165-195; *Concerning Rebaptism* (1528), 239-258; and *Preface to the Epistle of St. Paul to the Romans* (1522, rev. 1546), 98-107.

Luther, Martin, *Consolation to Those Women Who Have Had Difficulties in Bearing Children* (1) 1542, 179-182. In *Luther on Women, A Sourcebook*, translated by Susan C. Karant-Nunn and Merrie E. Wiesner-Hanks, 179-182 Cambridge: Cambridge University Press, 2003.

Pelikan, Jaroslav and Lehman, Helmut T., eds. *Luther's Works: American Edition*. Philadelphia: Fortress Press, 1957.

See especially *The Holy and Blessed Sacrament of Baptism* (1519), 35:45-73.

Wengert, Timothy and Kolb, Robert, eds. *The Book of Concord (New Translation): The Confessions of the Evangelical Lutheran Church* (Minneapolis: Fortress Press, 2000).

See especially *The Large Catechism* (1529), 377-480; *The Small Catechism*, (1529), 345-375; *Booklet on Baptism* (1523), 371-375; and *The Smalcald Articles*, (1537), 295-328.

For Further Reading on Luther's Theology and History of Baptism

Cramer, Peter. *Baptism in the Early Middle Ages, c. 200–c.1150.* Cambridge: Cambridge University Press, 1993.

Forde, Gerhard O. *The Preached God, Proclamation in Word and Sacrament.* Edited by Mark C. Mattes and Steven D. Paulson. Grand Rapids: Eerdmans, 2007.
    See especially the chapter titled "Something to Believe: A Theological Perspective on Infant Baptism," 131-45.

Hendrix, Scott. "Martin Luther's Reformation of Spirituality." In *Harvesting Martin Luther's Reflections on Theology, Ethics, and the Church*, 240–260. Edited by Timothy J. Wengert. Grand Rapids: Eerdmans, 2004.

Hinkle, Mary E. *Signs of Belonging: Luther's Marks of the Church and the Christian Life.* Minneapolis: Augsburg Fortress, 2003.

Mannermaa, Tuomo. *Christ Present in Faith: Luther's View of Justification.* Edited and introduced by Kirsi Stjerna. Minneapolis: Fortress Press, 2005.

Martin Luther Colloquium. *Luther, Baptism, and Christian Formation.* Papers presented at the ninth Martin Luther Colloquium at Lutheran Theological Seminary at Gettysburg, Pennsylvania, 1978. Published in Lutheran Theological Seminary at Gettysburg *Bulletin* 59, no. 1 (1978). Note: Today this event is known as the Luther Colloquy and this publication is known as *Seminary Ridge Review.*

Scaer, David. *Baptism.* St. Louis, Mo.: The Luther Academy, 1999.

Spinks, Bryan D. *Early and Medieval Rituals and Theologies of Baptism: From the New Testament to the Council of Trent,* vol 1. Burlington, Vt.: Ashgate, 2006.

Spinks, Bryan D. *Reformation and Modern Rituals and Theologies of Baptism: From Luther to Contemporary Practices,* vol 2. Burlington, Vt.: Ashgate, 2006.

Trigg, Jonathan. *Baptism in the Theology of Martin Luther.* Leiden: Brill Academic Publishers, 1994.

Wengert, Timothy J. "Luther on Children: Baptism and the Fourth Commandment." *Dialog* 37, no.3 (Summer 1998), 185-89.